80 Irish Recipes for Home

By: Kelly Johnson

Table of Contents

Appetizers:
- Irish Soda Bread with Smoked Salmon
- Boxty (Irish Potato Pancakes)
- Dublin Coddle Soup
- Irish Rarebit
- Colcannon Bites

Main Courses:
- Guinness Beef Stew
- Shepherd's Pie
- Corned Beef and Cabbage
- Dublin Lawyer (Lobster in Whiskey Cream Sauce)
- Irish Lamb Stew
- Bangers and Mash with Onion Gravy
- Irish Chicken Casserole
- Dublin Lawyer (Lobster in Whiskey Cream Sauce)
- Irish Whiskey Glazed Salmon
- Dublin Coddle (Sausage and Bacon Stew)

Sides:
- Champ (Mashed Potatoes with Green Onions)
- Boxty Dumplings
- Roasted Root Vegetables with Thyme
- Irish Colcannon
- Sautéed Cabbage with Bacon
- Irish Soda Bread Stuffing
- Buttered Parsnips
- Irish Potato Leek Soup
- Dublin Bay Prawns with Garlic Butter
- Boxty Fries

Desserts:
- Irish Apple Cake
- Baileys Irish Cream Cheesecake
- Traditional Irish Trifle
- Chocolate Guinness Cake
- Irish Whiskey Chocolate Fondue
- Carrageen Moss Pudding
- Irish Coffee Mousse
- Porter Cake
- Barmbrack (Irish Tea Bread)
- Irish Cream Profiteroles

Breads:
- Traditional Irish Soda Bread
- Brown Soda Bread
- Wheaten Bread
- Potato Farls
- Irish Barmbrack Bread

Breakfast:
- Irish Breakfast Fry-Up
- Boxty Breakfast Tacos
- Black Pudding and Apple Pancakes
- Porridge with Honey and Whiskey
- Irish Sausage Rolls

Beverages:
- Irish Coffee
- Black Velvet Cocktail
- Hot Whiskey
- Irish Cream Liqueur
- Dingle Gin and Tonic
- Redbreast Irish Whiskey Sour
- Poitín Punch
- Irish Stout Float
- Irish Breakfast Tea Punch
- Celtic Honey Mead

Soups:
- Irish Potato and Leek Soup
- Seafood Chowder
- Dublin Coddle Soup
- Irish Nettle Soup
- Colcannon Soup

Savory Pies:
- Traditional Steak and Guinness Pie
- Chicken and Mushroom Pie
- Irish Lamb Pie
- Dublin Lawyer Pie (Lobster and Whiskey)
- Vegetarian Irish Stout Pie

Vegetarian:
- Vegetarian Shepherd's Pie
- Colcannon Stuffed Bell Peppers
- Boxty with Mushroom and Spinach Filling
- Dublin Coddle with Vegetarian Sausages
- Irish Lentil Stew

Grilled Delights:
- Grilled Irish Sausages with Mustard Sauce
- Grilled Salmon with Irish Whiskey Glaze

- Irish Lamb Burgers with Mint Sauce
- Boxty Quesadillas with Dubliner Cheese
- Grilled Vegetable Skewers with Irish Herb Marinade

Festive Treats:

- Christmas Plum Pudding
- Irish Christmas Cake
- Chocolate Boxty Blintzes for Pancake Tuesday
- Boxty Griddle Scones for St. Bridgid's Day
- Irish Halloween Barmbrack

Appetizers:

Irish Soda Bread with Smoked Salmon:

Ingredients:

For the Irish Soda Bread:

- 4 cups all-purpose flour
- 1 teaspoon baking soda (bicarbonate of soda)
- 1 teaspoon salt
- 1 and 3/4 cups buttermilk

For Serving:

- Smoked salmon slices
- Cream cheese
- Fresh dill, chopped
- Lemon wedges

Instructions:

1. Preheat the Oven:

- Preheat your oven to 425°F (220°C).

2. Prepare the Dry Ingredients:

- In a large mixing bowl, combine the all-purpose flour, baking soda, and salt. Mix well.

3. Add Buttermilk:

- Make a well in the center of the dry ingredients. Pour the buttermilk into the well. Use a wooden spoon to mix until the dough comes together.

4. Knead the Dough:

- Turn the dough onto a floured surface and knead it lightly, just until it forms a round loaf. Avoid over-kneading, as it can make the bread tough.

5. Shape the Bread:

- Place the round loaf on a lightly floured baking sheet. Use a sharp knife to score a deep "X" on the top of the loaf. This helps the bread to bake evenly.

6. Bake:

- Bake in the preheated oven for about 15 minutes. Then reduce the oven temperature to 400°F (200°C) and continue baking for an additional 20-30 minutes, or until the bread is golden brown and sounds hollow when tapped on the bottom.

7. Cool:

- Allow the Irish Soda Bread to cool on a wire rack.

8. Serving:

- Once the bread has cooled, slice it into thick slices. Spread each slice with cream cheese, top with smoked salmon, and sprinkle with chopped fresh dill.

9. Garnish:

- Serve the smoked salmon-topped Irish Soda Bread slices with lemon wedges on the side for a burst of citrus flavor.

Enjoy your delicious Irish Soda Bread with Smoked Salmon! Feel free to customize the toppings and add other ingredients like capers or red onion for extra flavor.

Boxty (Irish Potato Pancakes):

Ingredients:

- 2 cups raw potatoes, peeled and grated
- 1 cup cooked mashed potatoes
- 1 cup all-purpose flour
- 1 cup buttermilk
- 1 egg
- 1 teaspoon baking soda
- Salt and pepper to taste
- Butter or oil for frying

Instructions:

1. Prepare the Potatoes:

- Grate the raw potatoes using a box grater or food processor. Place the grated potatoes in a clean kitchen towel and squeeze out any excess moisture.

2. Mix Ingredients:

- In a large bowl, combine the grated raw potatoes, mashed potatoes, flour, buttermilk, egg, baking soda, salt, and pepper. Mix until well combined. The consistency should be like a thick batter.

3. Let the Batter Rest:

- Allow the batter to rest for about 15-20 minutes. This helps the flour to absorb the liquid and gives a fluffier texture to the boxty.

4. Cook the Boxty:

- Heat a frying pan over medium heat and add a little butter or oil.
- Spoon the batter into the pan, forming pancakes of your desired size. Cook until golden brown on both sides, about 3-4 minutes per side.

5. Keep Warm:

- Once cooked, transfer the boxty to a plate and keep warm. Repeat the process with the remaining batter.

6. Serving Suggestions:

- Boxty is often served with various toppings or accompaniments. You can serve them with sour cream, smoked salmon, sautéed mushrooms, or a sprinkle of fresh herbs.

7. Enjoy:

- Serve the boxty warm and enjoy these traditional Irish potato pancakes!

Feel free to adjust the seasoning and toppings according to your preference. Boxty makes a delicious and versatile dish that can be enjoyed for breakfast, brunch, or as a side dish.

Dublin Coddle Soup:

Ingredients:

- 1 pound (about 450g) pork sausages
- 8 slices bacon, chopped
- 1 large onion, thinly sliced
- 2 cloves garlic, minced
- 4 large potatoes, peeled and diced
- 2 carrots, peeled and sliced
- 4 cups chicken or vegetable broth
- 1 bay leaf
- Salt and pepper to taste
- Fresh parsley, chopped (for garnish)

Instructions:

1. Brown the Sausages and Bacon:

- In a large soup pot over medium heat, brown the sausages and bacon until they are cooked through and slightly crispy. Remove them from the pot and set them aside.

2. Sauté Onions and Garlic:

- In the same pot, sauté the sliced onions and minced garlic until they become translucent.

3. Add Potatoes and Carrots:

- Add the diced potatoes and sliced carrots to the pot. Stir them in with the onions and garlic.

4. Combine with Broth:

- Pour in the chicken or vegetable broth, and add the bay leaf. Bring the mixture to a simmer.

5. Simmer:

- Allow the soup to simmer until the potatoes and carrots are tender, typically around 15-20 minutes.

6. Slice Sausages:

- While the soup is simmering, slice the cooked sausages into bite-sized pieces.

7. Add Sausages and Bacon:

- Once the vegetables are tender, add the sliced sausages and cooked bacon back into the pot. Stir to combine.

8. Season:

- Season the soup with salt and pepper to taste. Adjust the seasoning as needed.

9. Serve:

- Ladle the Dublin Coddle Soup into bowls. Garnish with chopped fresh parsley.

10. Enjoy:

- Serve the soup hot and enjoy this Irish-inspired dish!

Feel free to adjust the ingredients and seasoning according to your taste. This Dublin Coddle Soup is a warming and comforting option, perfect for a cold day.

Irish Rarebit:

Ingredients:

- 2 tablespoons unsalted butter
- 2 tablespoons all-purpose flour
- 1 teaspoon Dijon mustard
- 1 teaspoon Worcestershire sauce
- 1/2 teaspoon salt
- 1/4 teaspoon black pepper
- 1 cup Irish stout beer (like Guinness)
- 2 cups shredded sharp cheddar cheese
- 4 slices of thick bread, toasted
- Optional: Sliced tomatoes, cooked bacon, or poached eggs for topping

Instructions:

1. Make the Cheese Sauce:

   - In a saucepan over medium heat, melt the butter. Add the flour and whisk continuously for about 2 minutes to create a roux.

2. Add Flavorings:

   - Stir in the Dijon mustard, Worcestershire sauce, salt, and black pepper.

3. Pour in Beer:

   - Gradually pour in the Irish stout beer while whisking constantly to avoid lumps.

4. Melt Cheese:

   - Add the shredded cheddar cheese to the saucepan. Continue to whisk until the cheese is fully melted and the sauce is smooth and thickened.

5. Toast the Bread:

   - Toast the slices of bread under a broiler or in a toaster until they are golden brown.

6. Serve:

   - Pour the warm cheese sauce over the toasted bread slices.

7. Optional Toppings:

   - Garnish with sliced tomatoes, cooked bacon, or poached eggs if desired.

8. Broil (Optional):

   - If you want a bubbly, golden top, place the rarebit under the broiler for a minute or two until it's lightly browned.

9. Enjoy:

   - Serve the Irish Rarebit immediately while it's warm and gooey.

This dish is rich and flavorful, making it a delightful comfort food. Feel free to customize it with your favorite toppings or spices. Irish Rarebit is often enjoyed as a snack, light meal, or even as a brunch option.

Colcannon Bites:

Ingredients:

- 2 cups mashed potatoes (prepared without too much liquid)
- 1 cup finely chopped kale or cabbage, blanched and drained
- 1 cup shredded cheddar cheese
- 2 green onions, finely chopped
- 1 clove garlic, minced
- Salt and pepper to taste
- 1 cup breadcrumbs (for coating)
- 2 large eggs, beaten
- Cooking oil for frying

Instructions:

1. Prepare Mashed Potatoes:

   - Prepare mashed potatoes without adding too much liquid. You want a firm consistency that can hold its shape.

2. Blanch Kale or Cabbage:

   - Blanch the chopped kale or cabbage in boiling water for about 2-3 minutes. Drain well.

3. Combine Ingredients:

   - In a large mixing bowl, combine the mashed potatoes, blanched kale or cabbage, shredded cheddar cheese, chopped green onions, minced garlic, salt, and pepper. Mix well.

4. Shape the Bites:

   - Using your hands, shape the mixture into bite-sized balls or patties.

5. Coat in Breadcrumbs:

   - Dip each Colcannon bite into beaten eggs and then roll them in breadcrumbs, ensuring they are evenly coated.

6. Refrigerate (Optional):

   - For better firmness, you can refrigerate the bites for about 30 minutes.

7. Fry the Bites:

   - Heat cooking oil in a skillet over medium heat. Fry the Colcannon bites until they are golden brown on all sides.

8. Drain and Serve:

   - Place the fried bites on a paper towel-lined plate to drain any excess oil.

9. Garnish and Serve:

   - Optionally, garnish with additional chopped green onions or a dollop of sour cream. Serve the Colcannon Bites while they are still warm.

These Colcannon Bites are a delightful twist on the classic Irish dish, perfect for parties, appetizers, or even as a unique side dish. Adjust the seasonings and ingredients according to your taste preferences. Enjoy!

Main Courses:

Guinness Beef Stew:

Ingredients:

- 2 pounds (about 1 kg) stewing beef, cut into chunks
- Salt and black pepper to taste
- 3 tablespoons all-purpose flour
- 2 tablespoons vegetable oil
- 2 onions, chopped
- 3 cloves garlic, minced
- 2 tablespoons tomato paste
- 2 tablespoons all-purpose flour
- 2 cups (480 ml) beef broth
- 1 can (14.9 ounces / 440 ml) Guinness stout
- 2 bay leaves
- 1 teaspoon dried thyme
- 4 carrots, peeled and sliced
- 4 potatoes, peeled and diced
- Fresh parsley, chopped (for garnish)

Instructions:

1. Preheat the Oven:

- Preheat your oven to 325°F (163°C).

2. Season and Flour the Beef:

- Season the beef chunks with salt and black pepper. Toss the beef in 3 tablespoons of flour until evenly coated.

3. Brown the Beef:

- Heat the vegetable oil in a large oven-safe pot over medium-high heat. Brown the beef chunks in batches, ensuring they are seared on all sides. Remove the browned beef from the pot and set it aside.

4. Sauté Onions and Garlic:

   - In the same pot, add the chopped onions and sauté until they become translucent. Add minced garlic and cook for an additional minute.

5. Add Tomato Paste and Flour:

   - Stir in the tomato paste and 2 tablespoons of flour. Cook for 2-3 minutes to remove the raw taste of the flour.

6. Deglaze with Guinness:

   - Pour in the Guinness stout, scraping the bottom of the pot to release any flavorful bits stuck to it.

7. Add Broth and Seasonings:

   - Add the beef broth, bay leaves, and dried thyme. Return the browned beef chunks to the pot.

8. Simmer and Transfer to Oven:

   - Bring the mixture to a simmer. Once simmering, cover the pot and transfer it to the preheated oven. Bake for 2 hours.

9. Add Vegetables:

   - After 2 hours, add the sliced carrots and diced potatoes to the stew. Return the pot to the oven and bake for an additional 30-45 minutes or until the vegetables are tender.

10. Garnish and Serve:

    - Remove the bay leaves. Garnish the Guinness Beef Stew with chopped fresh parsley before serving.

This hearty and flavorful Guinness Beef Stew is perfect for a cozy and satisfying meal, especially on chilly days. Enjoy!

Shepherd's Pie:

Ingredients:

For the Filling:

- 1.5 pounds (about 700g) ground lamb or beef
- 1 onion, finely chopped
- 2 carrots, diced
- 2 cloves garlic, minced
- 2 tablespoons tomato paste
- 1 cup frozen peas
- 1 cup beef or vegetable broth
- 2 tablespoons all-purpose flour
- 1 teaspoon Worcestershire sauce
- Salt and pepper to taste
- Fresh thyme or rosemary (optional)

For the Mashed Potatoes:

- 4 large potatoes, peeled and diced
- 1/2 cup unsalted butter
- 1/2 cup milk
- Salt and pepper to taste
- Grated cheese (optional, for topping)

Instructions:

1. Prepare the Mashed Potatoes:

- Boil the peeled and diced potatoes until fork-tender. Drain and mash them with butter, milk, salt, and pepper until smooth. Set aside.

2. Cook the Meat Filling:

- In a large skillet, brown the ground lamb or beef over medium heat. Drain any excess fat.
- Add chopped onions, carrots, and minced garlic. Cook until the vegetables are softened.

3. Add Tomato Paste and Flour:

- Stir in the tomato paste and cook for a couple of minutes. Sprinkle the flour over the meat mixture and mix well.

4. Deglaze with Broth:

- Pour in the beef or vegetable broth and Worcestershire sauce. Stir to combine, allowing the mixture to thicken. Season with salt, pepper, and fresh herbs if desired.

5. Add Peas:

- Add the frozen peas to the meat mixture. Cook for a few minutes until everything is heated through.

6. Assemble the Pie:

- Preheat the oven to 400°F (200°C).
- Transfer the meat filling to a baking dish. Spread the mashed potatoes over the top, creating an even layer. Optionally, sprinkle grated cheese over the mashed potatoes.

7. Bake:

- Place the baking dish in the preheated oven and bake for about 20-25 minutes or until the top is golden brown.

8. Serve:

- Allow the Shepherd's Pie to cool for a few minutes before serving. Garnish with additional fresh herbs if desired.

This Shepherd's Pie is a hearty and satisfying dish, perfect for family dinners. Feel free to customize the recipe by adding other vegetables or herbs to suit your taste.

Corned Beef and Cabbage:

Ingredients:

- 3-4 pounds corned beef brisket
- 10 small red potatoes, quartered
- 5 carrots, peeled and cut into 3-inch pieces
- 1 large onion, peeled and cut into wedges
- 1 small cabbage, cored and cut into wedges
- 4 cloves garlic, minced
- 1 teaspoon whole black peppercorns
- 1 teaspoon mustard seeds
- 1 bay leaf
- Water, as needed

Instructions:

1. Prepare the Corned Beef:

   - Rinse the corned beef brisket under cold water to remove excess brine. Place it in a large pot.

2. Add Aromatics:

   - Add the minced garlic, black peppercorns, mustard seeds, and bay leaf to the pot.

3. Simmer:

   - Add enough water to the pot to cover the corned beef. Bring it to a boil, then reduce the heat to a simmer. Cover and simmer for about 2.5 to 3 hours or until the meat is tender.

4. Add Vegetables:

   - Add the quartered red potatoes, carrot pieces, onion wedges, and cabbage wedges to the pot during the last 30-40 minutes of cooking. This allows the vegetables to cook until tender.

5. Check for Doneness:

- Check the corned beef for tenderness. It should be fork-tender and easily pull apart.

6. Slice and Serve:

    - Remove the corned beef from the pot and let it rest for a few minutes before slicing. Slice against the grain for the most tender results.

7. Serve with Vegetables:

    - Arrange the sliced corned beef on a serving platter and surround it with the cooked vegetables.

8. Optional Sauce:

    - Serve with mustard or a horseradish sauce on the side if desired.

9. Enjoy:

    - Serve the Corned Beef and Cabbage hot and enjoy this traditional Irish-American dish.

This dish is not only popular for St. Patrick's Day but is also a hearty and flavorful meal any time of the year. Adjust the cooking time if you're using a slow cooker or Instant Pot for added convenience.

Dublin Lawyer (Lobster in Whiskey Cream Sauce):

Ingredients:

- 2 lobster tails (about 8-10 ounces each)
- 1/2 cup (1 stick) unsalted butter
- 2 cloves garlic, minced
- 1/4 cup Irish whiskey
- 1 cup heavy cream
- Salt and black pepper to taste
- Fresh parsley, chopped (for garnish)
- Lemon wedges (for serving)

Instructions:

1. Prepare the Lobster Tails:

   - Thaw the lobster tails if they are frozen. Remove the shells and cut the lobster meat into bite-sized pieces.

2. Sauté Lobster:

   - In a large skillet, melt the butter over medium heat. Add the minced garlic and sauté for about 1-2 minutes until fragrant.

3. Add Lobster:

   - Add the lobster pieces to the skillet and cook until they are opaque and cooked through, about 5-7 minutes. Remove the lobster from the skillet and set it aside.

4. Deglaze with Whiskey:

   - Pour the Irish whiskey into the skillet, deglazing the pan by scraping up any browned bits. Allow the whiskey to simmer for a couple of minutes to reduce slightly.

5. Add Cream:

- Pour in the heavy cream and stir to combine. Simmer for another 5 minutes until the sauce thickens.

6. Return Lobster:

- Return the cooked lobster pieces to the skillet, coating them evenly with the whiskey cream sauce. Cook for an additional 2-3 minutes until everything is heated through.

7. Season:

- Season the Dublin Lawyer with salt and black pepper to taste. Adjust the seasoning if needed.

8. Garnish and Serve:

- Garnish the dish with chopped fresh parsley. Serve the Dublin Lawyer hot with lemon wedges on the side.

9. Enjoy:

- Enjoy this indulgent and flavorful lobster dish with a side of crusty bread or over pasta.

Dublin Lawyer is a decadent treat, and the whiskey cream sauce adds a unique Irish twist to this seafood dish. It's perfect for a special occasion or a fancy dinner at home.

Irish Lamb Stew:

Ingredients:

- 2 pounds (about 1 kg) lamb stew meat, cut into chunks
- 2 tablespoons vegetable oil
- 3 tablespoons all-purpose flour
- Salt and black pepper to taste
- 2 large onions, chopped
- 3 cloves garlic, minced
- 4 carrots, peeled and sliced
- 4 celery stalks, sliced
- 1.5 pounds (about 700g) potatoes, peeled and diced
- 2 tablespoons tomato paste
- 1 teaspoon dried thyme
- 2 bay leaves
- 4 cups (about 1 liter) beef or lamb broth
- 1 cup (about 240 ml) red wine (optional)
- Chopped fresh parsley (for garnish)

Instructions:

1. Brown the Lamb:

- In a large pot or Dutch oven, heat the vegetable oil over medium-high heat. Season the lamb chunks with salt and pepper, then coat them in flour. Brown the lamb in batches to achieve a golden crust. Set aside.

2. Sauté Onions and Garlic:

- In the same pot, sauté the chopped onions until they become translucent. Add the minced garlic and cook for an additional minute.

3. Deglaze and Add Tomatoes:

- If using red wine, pour it into the pot to deglaze, scraping up any browned bits. Add the tomato paste and stir well.

4. Add Vegetables and Herbs:

- Return the browned lamb to the pot. Add carrots, celery, potatoes, dried thyme, and bay leaves. Mix everything together.

5. Pour in Broth:

- Pour in the beef or lamb broth until all the ingredients are submerged. Bring the stew to a simmer.

6. Simmer:

- Reduce the heat to low, cover the pot, and let the stew simmer for 1.5 to 2 hours or until the lamb is tender and the flavors meld.

7. Check Seasoning:

- Taste and adjust the seasoning, adding more salt and pepper if needed.

8. Serve:

- Ladle the Irish Lamb Stew into bowls, and garnish with chopped fresh parsley.

9. Enjoy:

- Serve the stew hot, perhaps with a side of crusty bread or Irish soda bread.

This Irish Lamb Stew is a comforting and nourishing dish, perfect for a family meal or a gathering with friends. Adjust the ingredients and seasonings according to your taste preferences.

Bangers and Mash with Onion Gravy:

Ingredients:

For Bangers:

- 8 pork sausages (traditional bangers if available)
- 1-2 tablespoons vegetable oil

For Mashed Potatoes:

- 2 pounds (about 1 kg) potatoes, peeled and cut into chunks
- 1/2 cup (1 stick) unsalted butter
- 1/2 to 1 cup milk (adjust to desired consistency)
- Salt and black pepper to taste

For Onion Gravy:

- 2 large onions, thinly sliced
- 2 tablespoons vegetable oil or butter
- 2 tablespoons all-purpose flour
- 2 cups beef or vegetable broth
- 1 tablespoon Worcestershire sauce
- Salt and black pepper to taste

Optional:

- Chopped fresh parsley for garnish

Instructions:

1. Cook the Sausages:

- In a large skillet over medium heat, add vegetable oil. Add the sausages and cook until browned on all sides and cooked through. This usually takes about 15-20 minutes.

2. Prepare Mashed Potatoes:

- While the sausages are cooking, boil the potatoes until tender. Drain and mash them with butter, milk, salt, and black pepper until smooth. Adjust the consistency with more milk if needed.

3. Make Onion Gravy:

    - In a separate pan, heat oil or butter over medium heat. Add the sliced onions and cook until softened and caramelized, about 10-15 minutes.
    - Sprinkle flour over the onions and stir for a couple of minutes to cook out the raw taste of the flour.
    - Gradually whisk in the beef or vegetable broth and Worcestershire sauce. Simmer the gravy until it thickens. Season with salt and black pepper to taste.

4. Serve:

    - Place a generous portion of mashed potatoes on each plate. Top with sausages and pour the onion gravy over the top.

5. Garnish:

    - Optionally, garnish with chopped fresh parsley for a burst of color and added flavor.

6. Enjoy:

    - Serve the Bangers and Mash with Onion Gravy immediately while everything is hot.

This dish is a comforting and satisfying meal, and the rich onion gravy adds a flavorful touch. It's a classic pub-style meal that's easy to make at home.

Irish Chicken Casserole:

Ingredients:

- 4 boneless, skinless chicken breasts, cut into bite-sized pieces
- Salt and black pepper to taste
- 2 tablespoons olive oil
- 1 large onion, chopped
- 2 carrots, peeled and sliced
- 2 celery stalks, sliced
- 2 cloves garlic, minced
- 1/4 cup all-purpose flour
- 2 cups chicken broth
- 1 cup milk
- 1 teaspoon dried thyme
- 1 cup frozen peas
- 1 cup mushrooms, sliced
- 4 cups cooked potatoes, mashed
- Chopped fresh parsley for garnish (optional)

Instructions:

1. Preheat the Oven:

- Preheat your oven to 375°F (190°C).

2. Cook Chicken:

- Season the chicken pieces with salt and black pepper. In a large skillet, heat olive oil over medium-high heat. Brown the chicken pieces on all sides. Remove from the skillet and set aside.

3. Sauté Vegetables:

- In the same skillet, add chopped onions, carrots, celery, and minced garlic. Sauté until the vegetables are softened.

4. Make Roux:

- Sprinkle flour over the vegetables and stir to form a roux. Cook for 1-2 minutes to remove the raw taste of the flour.

5. Add Liquids:

- Gradually add chicken broth and milk, stirring continuously to avoid lumps. Bring the mixture to a simmer, and let it thicken.

6. Season and Add Chicken Back:

- Season the sauce with dried thyme. Add the browned chicken pieces back to the skillet. Stir in frozen peas and sliced mushrooms. Simmer for a few minutes until the chicken is cooked through.

7. Assemble the Casserole:

- Transfer the chicken and vegetable mixture into a casserole dish.

8. Top with Mashed Potatoes:

- Spoon the mashed potatoes over the chicken mixture, spreading them evenly to cover.

9. Bake:

- Place the casserole dish in the preheated oven and bake for 25-30 minutes or until the top is golden brown and the filling is bubbling.

10. Garnish and Serve:

- If desired, garnish with chopped fresh parsley before serving.

11. Enjoy:

- Serve the Irish Chicken Casserole hot and enjoy this hearty and flavorful dish.

This Irish Chicken Casserole is a satisfying and wholesome meal, combining the richness of chicken and vegetables with a creamy sauce. It's perfect for a cozy family dinner.

Dublin Lawyer (Lobster in Whiskey Cream Sauce):

Ingredients:

- 2 lobsters (about 1.5 to 2 pounds each), cooked and meat removed
- 1/2 cup (1 stick) unsalted butter
- 4 cloves garlic, minced
- 1/4 cup Irish whiskey
- 1 cup heavy cream
- Salt and black pepper to taste
- Chopped fresh parsley (for garnish)
- Lemon wedges (for serving)

Instructions:

1. Prepare the Lobster:

- Cook the lobsters by boiling or steaming. Once cooked, remove the meat from the shells and cut it into bite-sized pieces. Set aside.

2. Cook the Garlic:

- In a large skillet or pan, melt the butter over medium heat. Add the minced garlic and sauté for about 1-2 minutes until fragrant.

3. Add Whiskey:

- Pour the Irish whiskey into the skillet and let it simmer for a minute or two to reduce slightly.

4. Add Cream:

- Pour in the heavy cream, stirring continuously. Simmer for another 3-5 minutes until the sauce thickens.

5. Add Lobster:

- Add the lobster meat to the skillet, coating it evenly with the whiskey cream sauce. Cook for an additional 2-3 minutes until the lobster is heated through.

6. Season:

- Season the dish with salt and black pepper to taste. Adjust the seasoning if needed.

7. Garnish:

- Garnish the Dublin Lawyer with chopped fresh parsley.

8. Serve:

- Serve the Dublin Lawyer hot, perhaps with a side of crusty bread or over pasta.

9. Enjoy:

- Enjoy this indulgent and flavorful lobster dish with a squeeze of lemon on top.

Dublin Lawyer is a luxurious and savory dish that combines the sweetness of lobster with the richness of the whiskey cream sauce. It's perfect for special occasions or when you want to treat yourself to a delicious meal.

Irish Whiskey Glazed Salmon:

Ingredients:

- 4 salmon fillets
- Salt and black pepper to taste
- 2 tablespoons olive oil

For the Irish Whiskey Glaze:

- 1/4 cup Irish whiskey
- 1/4 cup brown sugar
- 2 tablespoons Dijon mustard
- 2 tablespoons soy sauce
- 2 cloves garlic, minced
- 1 teaspoon grated fresh ginger
- 1 tablespoon olive oil (for cooking the glaze)

Optional Garnish:

- Chopped fresh parsley or green onions

Instructions:

1. Preheat the Oven:

- Preheat your oven to 375°F (190°C).

2. Season Salmon:

- Season the salmon fillets with salt and black pepper.

3. Sear the Salmon:

- In an oven-safe skillet, heat 2 tablespoons of olive oil over medium-high heat. Sear the salmon fillets, skin-side down, for about 2-3 minutes until golden brown.

4. Make the Glaze:

- In a small saucepan, combine Irish whiskey, brown sugar, Dijon mustard, soy sauce, minced garlic, and grated ginger. Heat over medium heat, stirring constantly until the sugar is dissolved.

5. Simmer the Glaze:

- Allow the glaze to simmer for 5-7 minutes or until it thickens slightly. Remove it from the heat.

6. Glaze the Salmon:

- Spoon a generous amount of the whiskey glaze over each salmon fillet, ensuring they are well-coated.

7. Bake:

- Transfer the skillet to the preheated oven and bake for about 10-15 minutes or until the salmon is cooked through. The cooking time may vary depending on the thickness of your fillets.

8. Optional Broil:

- If you like a caramelized top, you can place the skillet under the broiler for the last 2-3 minutes of cooking.

9. Garnish and Serve:

- Garnish the Irish Whiskey Glazed Salmon with chopped fresh parsley or green onions.

10. Enjoy:

- Serve the salmon hot, drizzled with any remaining glaze from the skillet.

This Irish Whiskey Glazed Salmon is a delicious and sophisticated dish that's perfect for a special dinner. The glaze adds a sweet and savory element to the salmon, creating a memorable flavor profile.

Dublin Coddle (Sausage and Bacon Stew):

Ingredients:

- 8 pork sausages
- 8 rashers of bacon, chopped
- 4 large potatoes, peeled and thickly sliced
- 2 large onions, sliced
- 2 cloves garlic, minced
- 2 cups chicken or vegetable broth
- Salt and black pepper to taste
- Fresh parsley, chopped (for garnish)

Instructions:

1. Preheat the Oven:

    - Preheat your oven to 350°F (175°C).

2. Brown the Sausages and Bacon:

    - In a large skillet, brown the sausages and bacon over medium heat. Once browned, transfer them to a plate.

3. Sauté Onions and Garlic:

    - In the same skillet, sauté the sliced onions until they become translucent. Add minced garlic and cook for an additional minute.

4. Assemble the Coddle:

    - In a large ovenproof dish, layer half of the sliced potatoes at the bottom. Place half of the sausages and bacon on top. Add half of the sautéed onions and garlic.

5. Repeat Layers:

    - Repeat the layering process with the remaining potatoes, sausages, bacon, onions, and garlic.

6. Season:

- Season each layer with salt and black pepper to taste.

7. Pour in Broth:

    - Pour the chicken or vegetable broth over the layers. The liquid should almost cover the ingredients.

8. Bake:

    - Cover the dish with a lid or aluminum foil and bake in the preheated oven for about 1.5 to 2 hours or until the potatoes are tender.

9. Garnish:

    - Before serving, garnish with chopped fresh parsley.

10. Enjoy:

    - Serve the Dublin Coddle hot, either on its own or with crusty bread.

This Dublin Coddle is a comforting and straightforward dish, perfect for a cozy meal on a cold day. The slow cooking process allows the flavors to meld together, creating a tasty and satisfying stew.

Sides:

Champ (Mashed Potatoes with Green Onions):

Ingredients:

- 4 large potatoes, peeled and cut into chunks
- 1 cup milk
- 1 bunch green onions (scallions), finely chopped
- 1/2 cup (1 stick) unsalted butter
- Salt and white pepper to taste

Instructions:

1. Boil the Potatoes:

   - Place the potato chunks in a large pot and cover them with cold water. Bring to a boil and simmer until the potatoes are fork-tender. Drain the potatoes.

2. Warm the Milk:

   - While the potatoes are cooking, heat the milk in a small saucepan. Be careful not to boil it; you just want it warm.

3. Mash the Potatoes:

   - Mash the drained potatoes in a large bowl. You can use a potato masher or a ricer for a smoother consistency.

4. Add Warm Milk:

   - Gradually pour in the warm milk while continuing to mash the potatoes. The warm milk helps create a creamier texture.

5. Add Butter:

   - Add half of the butter to the mashed potatoes and continue mashing until the butter is fully incorporated.

6. Incorporate Green Onions:

- Fold in the finely chopped green onions (scallions) into the mashed potatoes. Reserve some for garnish if desired.

7. Season:

- Season the champ with salt and white pepper to taste. Adjust the seasoning as needed.

8. Serve:

- Transfer the champ to a serving dish. Create a well in the center of the champ and add the remaining butter to melt into the well.

9. Garnish:

- Garnish the champ with additional chopped green onions if desired.

10. Enjoy:

- Serve the champ hot as a delicious and flavorful side dish.

Champ is a wonderful accompaniment to various meat dishes, especially those with rich gravies. Its simplicity highlights the natural flavors of the potatoes and the freshness of the green onions.

Boxty Dumplings:

Ingredients:

- 1 cup raw grated potatoes
- 1 cup mashed potatoes
- 1 cup all-purpose flour
- 1 teaspoon baking powder
- Salt and black pepper to taste
- 1/2 cup buttermilk
- 1 tablespoon melted butter
- Chopped fresh herbs (such as parsley or chives, optional)

Instructions:

1. Prepare the Potatoes:

- Peel and grate raw potatoes. Squeeze out excess moisture using a clean kitchen towel or paper towel. Also, prepare mashed potatoes.

2. Mix Ingredients:

- In a large bowl, combine the grated raw potatoes, mashed potatoes, all-purpose flour, baking powder, salt, and black pepper.

3. Add Wet Ingredients:

- Pour in the buttermilk and melted butter. Mix the ingredients well to form a thick batter. If the batter is too dry, you can add a little more buttermilk.

4. Optional: Add Herbs:

- Optionally, add chopped fresh herbs, such as parsley or chives, to the batter for added flavor.

5. Shape Dumplings:

- With floured hands, shape the batter into golf ball-sized dumplings. Roll them between your palms to create smooth balls.

6. Cook Dumplings:

- Bring a pot of salted water to a gentle simmer. Drop the dumplings into the simmering water. Cook for about 15-20 minutes or until the dumplings are cooked through. They will float to the surface when done.

7. Serve:

- Once cooked, remove the dumplings with a slotted spoon and serve them hot.

8. Optional: Brown in Butter:

- For extra flavor, you can brown the cooked dumplings in a skillet with some butter until they develop a golden crust.

9. Enjoy:

- Serve the Boxty Dumplings on their own or as a delicious accompaniment to stews and soups.

Boxty Dumplings are a tasty way to enjoy the traditional Irish boxty in a different form. Their versatility makes them a great addition to various dishes, adding a potato-rich and comforting element to your meals.

Roasted Root Vegetables with Thyme:

Ingredients:

- 4 cups mixed root vegetables, peeled and diced (carrots, parsnips, sweet potatoes, turnips, and beets)
- 2 tablespoons olive oil
- 2 tablespoons fresh thyme leaves (or 1 tablespoon dried thyme)
- Salt and black pepper to taste
- Optional: 2-3 cloves garlic, minced
- Optional: Balsamic glaze for drizzling (optional)

Instructions:

1. Preheat the Oven:

- Preheat your oven to 400°F (200°C).

2. Prepare the Vegetables:

- Peel and dice the root vegetables into similar-sized pieces. This ensures even cooking.

3. Season the Vegetables:

- In a large bowl, toss the diced vegetables with olive oil, fresh thyme leaves, salt, black pepper, and minced garlic if using. Ensure the vegetables are well-coated.

4. Arrange on a Baking Sheet:

- Spread the seasoned vegetables in a single layer on a baking sheet. This allows them to roast evenly.

5. Roast in the Oven:

- Place the baking sheet in the preheated oven and roast for about 25-35 minutes or until the vegetables are tender and golden brown. Stir the vegetables halfway through the cooking time for even roasting.

6. Optional: Drizzle with Balsamic Glaze:

- If desired, drizzle the roasted root vegetables with balsamic glaze for an extra layer of flavor.

7. Serve:

- Transfer the roasted root vegetables to a serving dish and serve hot.

8. Enjoy:

- Enjoy the delicious combination of sweet and savory flavors from the roasted root vegetables with thyme.

This dish is not only flavorful but also visually appealing, making it a perfect side for various meals. The roasting process caramelizes the natural sugars in the vegetables, enhancing their sweetness. The addition of thyme adds a delightful herbal note to the overall taste.

Irish Colcannon:

Ingredients:

- 4 large potatoes, peeled and cut into chunks
- 4 cups shredded kale or cabbage
- 1 cup milk or cream (or a combination of both)
- 1/2 cup (1 stick) unsalted butter, divided
- Salt and black pepper to taste
- Optional: 4 green onions (scallions), finely chopped

Instructions:

1. Cook Potatoes:

- Place the potato chunks in a pot of cold salted water. Bring to a boil and simmer until the potatoes are fork-tender. Drain well.

2. Cook Kale or Cabbage:

- In a separate pot, blanch the shredded kale or cabbage in boiling water for about 3-5 minutes or until tender. Drain and set aside.

3. Mash Potatoes:

- Mash the cooked potatoes using a potato masher or a ricer for a smoother texture.

4. Heat Milk or Cream:

- In a small saucepan, heat the milk or cream (or a combination of both) until warmed. Be careful not to boil it.

5. Combine Ingredients:

- Add half of the butter to the mashed potatoes. Gradually pour in the warmed milk/cream, stirring continuously, until you achieve the desired creamy consistency.

6. Add Kale or Cabbage:

- Fold in the blanched kale or cabbage into the mashed potatoes. If using green onions, add them at this stage as well.

7. Season:

    - Season the colcannon with salt and black pepper to taste. Adjust the seasoning as needed.

8. Serve:

    - Transfer the colcannon to a serving dish. Make a well in the center and add the remaining butter to melt.

9. Enjoy:

    - Serve the Irish Colcannon hot as a delicious and comforting side dish.

Colcannon is a versatile dish that can be customized based on personal preferences. It's often served alongside traditional Irish meals, especially during holidays like St. Patrick's Day. The combination of creamy mashed potatoes with hearty greens makes it a wholesome and satisfying dish.

Sautéed Cabbage with Bacon:

Ingredients:

- 1 medium-sized cabbage, thinly sliced
- 6 slices of bacon, chopped
- 1 onion, finely chopped
- 2 cloves garlic, minced
- 2 tablespoons olive oil
- Salt and black pepper to taste
- Optional: Red pepper flakes for a hint of spice
- Fresh parsley, chopped (for garnish)

Instructions:

1. Prep the Ingredients:

- Thinly slice the cabbage, chop the bacon, finely chop the onion, and mince the garlic.

2. Cook Bacon:

- In a large skillet or pan, cook the chopped bacon over medium heat until it becomes crispy. Remove some of the excess bacon fat if there's too much, leaving about 1-2 tablespoons in the pan.

3. Sauté Onion and Garlic:

- Add the finely chopped onion to the skillet and sauté until it becomes translucent. Add the minced garlic and cook for an additional minute until fragrant.

4. Add Cabbage:

- Add the thinly sliced cabbage to the skillet, tossing it with the bacon, onion, and garlic. Drizzle olive oil over the cabbage.

5. Sauté:

- Sauté the cabbage over medium-high heat, stirring occasionally, until it wilts and becomes tender. This should take about 8-10 minutes.

6. Season:

- Season the sautéed cabbage with salt, black pepper, and red pepper flakes (if using). Adjust the seasoning according to your taste.

7. Garnish:

- Garnish the dish with chopped fresh parsley for a burst of freshness.

8. Serve:

- Serve the Sautéed Cabbage with Bacon hot as a flavorful side dish or a light main course.

9. Enjoy:

- Enjoy the combination of the savory bacon with the tender-crisp cabbage. This dish pairs well with a variety of mains and is quick to prepare.

Sautéed Cabbage with Bacon is a comforting and easy-to-make dish that brings out the natural sweetness of cabbage while adding a smoky flavor from the bacon. It's a perfect side for a weeknight dinner or a festive meal.

Irish Soda Bread Stuffing:

Ingredients:

- 1 loaf of Irish soda bread, diced into cubes (homemade or store-bought)
- 1/2 cup (1 stick) unsalted butter
- 1 large onion, diced
- 2 stalks celery, diced
- 2-3 cloves garlic, minced
- 1 teaspoon dried thyme
- 1 teaspoon dried sage
- Salt and black pepper to taste
- 1 1/2 to 2 cups chicken or vegetable broth
- Fresh parsley, chopped (for garnish, optional)

Instructions:

1. Preheat the Oven:

- Preheat your oven to 350°F (175°C).

2. Toast Irish Soda Bread Cubes:

- Spread the diced Irish soda bread cubes on a baking sheet. Toast them in the preheated oven for about 10-15 minutes or until they are slightly crisp. This step helps prevent the stuffing from becoming too mushy.

3. Sauté Vegetables:

- In a large skillet, melt the butter over medium heat. Add diced onion and celery. Sauté until the vegetables are softened, about 5-7 minutes. Add minced garlic and continue cooking for another minute.

4. Season:

- Stir in dried thyme, dried sage, salt, and black pepper. Adjust the seasoning according to your taste.

5. Combine with Soda Bread Cubes:

- In a large mixing bowl, combine the toasted Irish soda bread cubes with the sautéed vegetable mixture. Toss everything together until well combined.

6. Moisten with Broth:

- Gradually pour the chicken or vegetable broth over the bread and vegetable mixture. Gently toss until the mixture is moistened. Add enough broth to achieve the desired level of moisture.

7. Transfer to a Baking Dish:

- Transfer the stuffing mixture to a greased baking dish.

8. Bake:

- Bake in the preheated oven for 30-40 minutes or until the top is golden brown and the stuffing is heated through.

9. Garnish:

- If desired, garnish the Irish Soda Bread Stuffing with chopped fresh parsley before serving.

10. Serve:

- Serve the stuffing hot as a delicious and unique side dish for your holiday meals or special occasions.

This Irish Soda Bread Stuffing adds a wonderful twist to your holiday table with its distinct flavor and texture. It complements roast poultry or pork beautifully, and the toasted soda bread provides a deliciously hearty base for the stuffing.

Buttered Parsnips:

Ingredients:

- 4 large parsnips, peeled and sliced into even-sized sticks
- 2 tablespoons unsalted butter
- Salt and black pepper to taste
- Chopped fresh parsley (optional, for garnish)

Instructions:

1. Prepare Parsnips:

- Peel the parsnips and cut them into even-sized sticks, similar to the size of French fries.

2. Steam or Boil Parsnips:

- Steam or boil the parsnip sticks until they are just tender. This usually takes about 8-10 minutes. Test the doneness by inserting a fork; they should be easily pierced but still have a slight firmness.

3. Drain and Dry:

- If you boiled the parsnips, drain them well. It's essential to remove excess water to ensure a buttery coating.

4. Butter the Parsnips:

- In a large skillet, melt the butter over medium heat. Add the parsnip sticks to the skillet and toss them to coat evenly in the melted butter.

5. Sauté:

- Sauté the parsnips for a few minutes, allowing them to absorb the butter and develop a golden brown color. Stir occasionally to ensure even coating.

6. Season:

- Season the buttered parsnips with salt and black pepper to taste. Adjust the seasoning according to your preference.

7. Garnish:

- If desired, garnish the buttered parsnips with chopped fresh parsley for a pop of color and freshness.

8. Serve:

- Transfer the buttered parsnips to a serving dish and serve hot.

9. Enjoy:

- Enjoy these buttered parsnips as a delightful and simple side dish that complements a variety of main courses.

Buttered parsnips are a classic and comforting side dish that pairs well with roasted meats, poultry, or even as part of a vegetarian meal. The butter enhances the natural sweetness of the parsnips, making them a flavorful addition to your dinner table.

Irish Potato Leek Soup:

Ingredients:

- 2 tablespoons unsalted butter
- 3 leeks, white and light green parts only, cleaned and sliced
- 3 large potatoes, peeled and diced
- 4 cups vegetable or chicken broth
- Salt and black pepper to taste
- 1 cup milk or cream
- Chopped fresh chives or parsley (for garnish, optional)

Instructions:

1. Prepare Leeks:

- Clean the leeks thoroughly to remove any sand or dirt. Slice the leeks, using only the white and light green parts.

2. Sauté Leeks:

- In a large pot, melt the butter over medium heat. Add the sliced leeks and cook until softened, about 5-7 minutes.

3. Add Potatoes:

- Add the diced potatoes to the pot and stir to coat them with the butter and leeks.

4. Pour in Broth:

- Pour in the vegetable or chicken broth, ensuring that the potatoes are submerged. Bring the mixture to a simmer.

5. Simmer:

- Reduce the heat to low, cover the pot, and let the soup simmer for about 15-20 minutes or until the potatoes are tender.

6. Blend:

- Use an immersion blender to puree the soup until smooth. Alternatively, transfer the soup in batches to a blender and blend until smooth. Be cautious as the soup will be hot.

7. Season:

- Season the soup with salt and black pepper to taste. Adjust the seasoning as needed.

8. Add Milk or Cream:

- Pour in the milk or cream, stirring continuously. Allow the soup to heat through without boiling.

9. Garnish:

- If desired, garnish the Irish Potato Leek Soup with chopped fresh chives or parsley for a burst of color and added flavor.

10. Serve:

- Ladle the soup into bowls and serve hot. Optionally, you can drizzle with a bit of extra cream or sprinkle with more herbs.

11. Enjoy:

- Enjoy this hearty and creamy Irish Potato Leek Soup as a comforting appetizer or a light meal.

Irish Potato Leek Soup is a classic dish that warms the soul. Its velvety texture and delicate flavors make it a perfect choice for a cozy dinner, especially during colder months.

Dublin Bay Prawns with Garlic Butter:

Ingredients:

- 1 pound (450g) Dublin Bay prawns (or large shrimp), peeled and deveined
- 1/2 cup (1 stick) unsalted butter
- 4 cloves garlic, minced
- 2 tablespoons fresh parsley, chopped
- Salt and black pepper to taste
- Lemon wedges for serving

Instructions:

1. Prepare the Prawns:

- Ensure the Dublin Bay prawns are peeled and deveined. You can leave the tails on for presentation, if desired.

2. Melt Butter:

- In a large skillet or pan, melt the butter over medium heat.

3. Sauté Garlic:

- Add the minced garlic to the melted butter and sauté for 1-2 minutes until fragrant. Be careful not to let the garlic brown.

4. Cook the Prawns:

- Add the prawns to the skillet, tossing them in the garlic butter. Cook for 2-3 minutes per side or until the prawns turn pink and opaque. The cooking time may vary depending on the size of the prawns.

5. Season:

- Season the prawns with salt and black pepper to taste. Adjust the seasoning according to your preference.

6. Add Fresh Parsley:

- Sprinkle the fresh chopped parsley over the prawns, tossing them to coat evenly.

7. Serve:

- Transfer the Dublin Bay prawns with garlic butter to a serving dish.

8. Garnish:

- Garnish with additional fresh parsley if desired.

9. Serve with Lemon Wedges:

- Serve the prawns hot with lemon wedges on the side for a burst of citrus flavor.

10. Enjoy:

- Enjoy Dublin Bay Prawns with Garlic Butter as a delightful appetizer or as part of a seafood feast.

This dish is not only quick and easy to prepare but also showcases the sweet and succulent flavor of fresh prawns. The garlic butter adds richness and depth to the dish, making it a perfect treat for seafood lovers.

Boxty Fries:

Ingredients:

- 2 large russet potatoes, peeled and grated
- 1 cup mashed potatoes
- 1 cup all-purpose flour
- 1 teaspoon baking powder
- 1 teaspoon salt
- 1/2 cup buttermilk
- 2 tablespoons unsalted butter, melted
- Vegetable oil (for frying)
- Salt and black pepper to taste
- Optional: Chopped fresh herbs (such as parsley or chives) for garnish

Instructions:

1. Prepare the Potatoes:

- Peel and grate the russet potatoes. Squeeze out any excess moisture using a clean kitchen towel.

2. Mix Ingredients:

- In a large mixing bowl, combine the grated potatoes, mashed potatoes, all-purpose flour, baking powder, salt, buttermilk, and melted butter. Mix until well combined.

3. Form into Fries:

- Shape the mixture into fry-like shapes, forming them into sticks or using a scoop to create portions.

4. Heat Vegetable Oil:

   - In a deep fryer or a large, deep skillet, heat vegetable oil to 350°F (180°C).

5. Fry the Boxty Fries:

   - Carefully place the shaped boxty fries into the hot oil, working in batches to avoid overcrowding. Fry until golden brown and crispy, about 3-4 minutes per batch.

6. Drain and Season:

   - Remove the boxty fries from the oil using a slotted spoon and place them on a paper towel-lined plate to drain excess oil. Season with salt and black pepper immediately.

7. Garnish:

   - If desired, garnish the boxty fries with chopped fresh herbs like parsley or chives.

8. Serve:

   - Serve the Boxty Fries hot as a unique and flavorful side dish or snack.

9. Enjoy:

   - Enjoy the crispy exterior and tender interior of these boxty fries, a delightful twist on traditional potato fries.

Boxty Fries are a creative and delicious way to enjoy the flavors of boxty in a different form. They make for a great appetizer, side dish, or snack, and the crispy texture will be a hit with anyone who loves potatoes.

Desserts:

Irish Apple Cake:

Ingredients:

For the Cake:

- 2 cups all-purpose flour
- 1 teaspoon baking powder
- 1/4 teaspoon baking soda
- 1/2 cup unsalted butter, softened
- 1 cup granulated sugar
- 2 large eggs
- 1/2 cup milk
- 2 cups apples, peeled, cored, and diced
- 1 teaspoon ground cinnamon
- 1/4 teaspoon ground nutmeg
- 1/4 teaspoon salt

For the Topping:

- 2 tablespoons granulated sugar
- 1/2 teaspoon ground cinnamon

Instructions:

1. Preheat the Oven:

- Preheat your oven to 350°F (175°C). Grease and flour a round cake pan (8 or 9 inches).

2. Prepare the Dry Ingredients:

- In a medium bowl, whisk together the flour, baking powder, baking soda, cinnamon, nutmeg, and salt. Set aside.

3. Cream Butter and Sugar:

- In a large mixing bowl, cream together the softened butter and sugar until light and fluffy.

4. Add Eggs:

- Add the eggs one at a time, beating well after each addition.

5. Alternate Flour and Milk:

- Gradually add the dry ingredients to the butter mixture, alternating with the milk. Begin and end with the dry ingredients. Mix until just combined.

6. Fold in Apples:

- Gently fold in the diced apples until evenly distributed throughout the batter.

7. Transfer to Pan:

- Pour the batter into the prepared cake pan and spread it evenly.

8. Prepare Topping:

- In a small bowl, mix together the sugar and cinnamon for the topping.

9. Sprinkle Topping:

- Sprinkle the cinnamon-sugar mixture evenly over the top of the cake batter.

10. Bake:

    - Bake in the preheated oven for approximately 45-50 minutes, or until a toothpick inserted into the center comes out clean.

11. Cool:

    - Allow the cake to cool in the pan for about 10 minutes, then transfer it to a wire rack to cool completely.

12. Serve:

    - Once cooled, slice and serve the Irish Apple Cake. It's delicious on its own or with a dollop of whipped cream or a scoop of vanilla ice cream.

13. Enjoy:

    - Enjoy this moist and flavorful Irish Apple Cake, perfect for any occasion or a cozy dessert after a meal.

Irish Apple Cake is a classic treat that brings out the sweetness of apples in a simple and delicious way. The combination of cinnamon, nutmeg, and diced apples creates a delightful dessert that's perfect for sharing.

Baileys Irish Cream Cheesecake:

Ingredients:

For the Crust:

- 1 1/2 cups graham cracker crumbs
- 1/4 cup granulated sugar
- 1/2 cup unsalted butter, melted

For the Cheesecake Filling:

- 4 packages (32 ounces total) cream cheese, softened
- 1 cup granulated sugar
- 4 large eggs
- 1 cup Baileys Irish Cream
- 1 teaspoon vanilla extract
- 1/4 cup all-purpose flour

For the Baileys Ganache:

- 1/2 cup heavy cream
- 1 cup semi-sweet chocolate chips
- 2 tablespoons Baileys Irish Cream

Instructions:

1. Preheat the Oven:

- Preheat your oven to 325°F (163°C). Grease a 9-inch springform pan.

2. Prepare the Crust:

- In a medium bowl, combine graham cracker crumbs, sugar, and melted butter. Press the mixture into the bottom of the prepared springform pan. Bake the crust in the preheated oven for about 10 minutes. Remove and allow it to cool while you prepare the filling.

3. Make the Cheesecake Filling:

- In a large mixing bowl, beat the softened cream cheese until smooth and creamy. Add the sugar and continue to beat until well combined.

4. Add Eggs and Flavorings:

- Add the eggs one at a time, beating well after each addition. Mix in the Baileys Irish Cream and vanilla extract.

5. Incorporate Flour:

- Gradually add the flour to the cream cheese mixture and mix until just combined. Be careful not to overmix.

6. Pour into Crust:

- Pour the cheesecake batter over the prepared crust in the springform pan.

7. Bake:

- Bake the cheesecake in the preheated oven for approximately 60-70 minutes, or until the center is set and the top is lightly browned. The center may still be slightly jiggly, but it will firm up as it cools.

8. Cool and Refrigerate:

- Allow the cheesecake to cool in the pan for about 1 hour, then refrigerate for at least 4 hours or overnight to chill and set.

9. Make the Baileys Ganache:

- In a small saucepan, heat the heavy cream over medium heat until it just begins to simmer. Remove from heat and add the chocolate chips and Baileys Irish Cream. Stir until smooth and well combined.

10. Pour Ganache over Cheesecake:

- Pour the Baileys ganache over the chilled cheesecake, spreading it evenly.

11. Chill Again:

- Return the cheesecake to the refrigerator and allow it to chill for an additional 1-2 hours to set the ganache.

12. Serve:

- Once fully chilled and set, run a knife around the edge of the springform pan and release the sides. Slice and serve the Baileys Irish Cream Cheesecake.

13. Enjoy:

- Enjoy this indulgent dessert with the rich and creamy flavors of Baileys Irish Cream!

This Baileys Irish Cream Cheesecake is a perfect treat for special occasions or when you want to savor a luxurious and flavorful dessert.

Traditional Irish Trifle:

Ingredients:

For the Sponge Cake:

- 1 store-bought sponge cake or homemade sponge cake, cut into cubes

For the Custard:

- 2 cups whole milk
- 1 cup heavy cream
- 1 teaspoon vanilla extract
- 6 large egg yolks
- 1/2 cup granulated sugar
- 1/4 cup cornstarch

For the Fruit Layer:

- 2 cups mixed berries (strawberries, blueberries, raspberries)
- 2 tablespoons sugar (optional, for macerating the berries)

For Whipped Cream:

- 1 cup heavy cream
- 2 tablespoons powdered sugar
- 1 teaspoon vanilla extract

For Garnish:

- Sliced almonds or grated chocolate (optional)

Instructions:

1. Prepare the Custard:

- In a saucepan, heat the milk and heavy cream over medium heat until it just begins to simmer. Remove from heat and stir in the vanilla extract.
- In a separate bowl, whisk together the egg yolks, sugar, and cornstarch until well combined.

- Slowly pour the warm milk mixture into the egg mixture, whisking continuously to avoid curdling.
- Return the mixture to the saucepan and cook over medium heat, stirring constantly, until the custard thickens. This will take about 5-7 minutes. Remove from heat and let it cool.

2. Prepare the Fruit:

- If desired, toss the mixed berries with sugar to macerate them. Let them sit for about 15-30 minutes to release their juices.

3. Make the Whipped Cream:

- In a chilled bowl, whip the heavy cream, powdered sugar, and vanilla extract until stiff peaks form.

4. Assemble the Trifle:

- In a trifle dish or a glass bowl, start by layering the sponge cake cubes at the bottom.
- Pour a layer of custard over the sponge cake.
- Add a layer of macerated berries.
- Repeat the layers until you reach the top of the trifle dish, finishing with a layer of whipped cream on top.

5. Garnish:

- Garnish the trifle with sliced almonds or grated chocolate, if desired.

6. Chill:

- Refrigerate the trifle for at least 2-3 hours, allowing the flavors to meld and the dessert to chill.

7. Serve:

- Serve the Traditional Irish Trifle chilled, scooping out portions that include all the delicious layers.

8. Enjoy:

- Enjoy this classic Irish dessert with its layers of sponge cake, custard, fruit, and whipped cream.

Irish Trifle is not only a visually appealing dessert but also a crowd-pleaser with its combination of textures and flavors. It's a perfect treat for celebrations or special occasions.

Chocolate Guinness Cake:

Ingredients:

For the Cake:

- 1 cup Guinness stout
- 1 cup unsalted butter, cubed
- 3/4 cup unsweetened cocoa powder
- 2 cups all-purpose flour
- 2 cups granulated sugar
- 1 1/2 teaspoons baking soda
- 3/4 teaspoon salt
- 2 large eggs
- 2/3 cup sour cream

For the Cream Cheese Frosting:

- 8 oz (225g) cream cheese, softened
- 1 1/2 cups powdered sugar
- 1/2 cup heavy cream
- 1 teaspoon vanilla extract

Instructions:

1. Preheat the Oven:

- Preheat your oven to 350°F (175°C). Grease and line a 9-inch round cake pan.

2. Prepare the Cake Batter:

- In a saucepan, heat the Guinness and butter over medium heat until the butter is melted. Whisk in the cocoa powder until smooth. Remove from heat and let it cool slightly.
- In a large mixing bowl, whisk together the flour, sugar, baking soda, and salt.
- In a separate bowl, beat the eggs and sour cream. Add this mixture to the dry ingredients and mix well.
- Pour in the Guinness and cocoa mixture, and stir until the batter is smooth and well combined.

3. Bake the Cake:

- Pour the batter into the prepared cake pan. Bake in the preheated oven for 45-50 minutes or until a toothpick inserted into the center comes out clean.

4. Cool the Cake:

- Allow the cake to cool in the pan for about 15 minutes, then transfer it to a wire rack to cool completely.

5. Prepare the Cream Cheese Frosting:

- In a bowl, beat the softened cream cheese until smooth. Add powdered sugar, heavy cream, and vanilla extract. Beat until the frosting is smooth and well combined.

6. Frost the Cake:

- Once the cake is completely cooled, spread the cream cheese frosting over the top. You can also frost the sides if desired.

7. Serve:

- Slice and serve the Chocolate Guinness Cake.

8. Enjoy:

- Enjoy this rich and moist chocolate cake with the unique depth of flavor from Guinness beer.

The Chocolate Guinness Cake is a perfect dessert for St. Patrick's Day or any celebration where you want to indulge in a decadent treat. The combination of chocolate and beer creates a moist and flavorful cake, and the cream cheese frosting adds a delicious finishing touch.

Irish Whiskey Chocolate Fondue:

Ingredients:

- 8 ounces (about 225g) good quality dark chocolate, finely chopped
- 1/2 cup heavy cream
- 2 tablespoons unsalted butter
- 2 tablespoons Irish whiskey
- Assorted dippables: strawberries, banana slices, marshmallows, pretzels, cubes of pound cake, etc.

Instructions:

1. Prepare the Chocolate:

- Place the finely chopped dark chocolate in a heatproof bowl.

2. Heat the Cream:

- In a small saucepan, heat the heavy cream and butter over medium heat until it just starts to simmer. Do not boil.

3. Melt the Chocolate:

- Pour the hot cream and butter mixture over the chopped chocolate. Let it sit for a minute to allow the chocolate to melt.
- Gently stir the mixture until the chocolate is completely melted and smooth.

4. Add Irish Whiskey:

- Stir in the Irish whiskey until well combined with the chocolate mixture.

5. Set Up the Fondue Pot:

- If you have a fondue pot, transfer the chocolate mixture to the pot and set it over low heat to keep the chocolate warm. If not, you can use a heatproof bowl over a tea light or low flame.

6. Arrange Dippables:

- Arrange the assorted dippables on a serving platter. Get creative with your choices!

7. Dip and Enjoy:

- Invite everyone to dip their favorite items into the warm Irish Whiskey Chocolate Fondue. Use fondue forks or skewers for easy dipping.

8. Keep Warm:

- Keep the fondue warm throughout the serving time by adjusting the heat source or reheating gently if needed.

9. Enjoy:

- Enjoy this indulgent and spirited dessert with friends and family.

Irish Whiskey Chocolate Fondue is a fun and social dessert that's perfect for entertaining. The combination of rich chocolate and the warmth of Irish whiskey adds a delightful twist to the traditional fondue experience.

Carrageen Moss Pudding:

Ingredients:

- 1/4 cup dried carrageen moss
- 4 cups milk
- 1/4 cup sugar
- 1 teaspoon vanilla extract
- Ground cinnamon or nutmeg (for garnish, optional)

Instructions:

1. Prepare Carrageen Moss:

- Rinse the dried carrageen moss thoroughly under cold running water to remove any impurities.
- Soak the carrageen moss in a bowl of cold water for about 15-20 minutes.

2. Strain Carrageen Moss:

- Strain the carrageen moss, discarding the soaking water.

3. Simmer in Milk:

- In a saucepan, heat the milk over medium heat until it almost comes to a boil.
- Add the strained carrageen moss to the milk, reduce the heat to low, and simmer gently for about 15-20 minutes. Stir occasionally.

4. Sweeten the Pudding:

- Add sugar to the milk and carrageen moss mixture, stirring until the sugar is fully dissolved.

- Continue to simmer for an additional 5-10 minutes, allowing the carrageen moss to fully dissolve and thicken the pudding.

5. Remove from Heat:

- Remove the saucepan from the heat and let the mixture cool slightly.

6. Add Vanilla:

- Stir in the vanilla extract, ensuring it is well incorporated into the pudding.

7. Strain (Optional):

- If desired, strain the pudding through a fine mesh sieve to remove any remaining bits of carrageen moss. This step is optional, as some people prefer the texture of the moss in the pudding.

8. Pour into Molds:

- Pour the pudding mixture into individual molds or a large serving dish.

9. Chill:

- Allow the Carrageen Moss Pudding to cool to room temperature before refrigerating it. Let it chill in the refrigerator for at least 4 hours or until set.

10. Garnish and Serve:

- Before serving, sprinkle the top of the pudding with ground cinnamon or nutmeg, if desired.

11. Enjoy:

- Serve chilled and enjoy this unique Irish dessert.

Carrageen Moss Pudding has a delicate flavor and a smooth, creamy texture. It's a traditional Irish treat that connects to the country's coastal heritage. The carrageen moss acts as a natural thickening agent, creating a pudding with a consistency similar to panna cotta.

Irish Coffee Mousse:

Ingredients:

- 1 cup strong brewed coffee, cooled
- 1 tablespoon instant coffee granules (optional, for extra coffee flavor)
- 3 tablespoons Irish whiskey
- 3 large egg yolks
- 1/2 cup granulated sugar
- 1 1/2 cups heavy cream
- Cocoa powder or chocolate shavings (for garnish, optional)

Instructions:

1. Brew Strong Coffee:

- Brew a cup of strong coffee and let it cool to room temperature.

2. Dissolve Instant Coffee (Optional):

- If you want an extra kick of coffee flavor, dissolve instant coffee granules in a small amount of hot water and add them to the brewed coffee. Stir well.

3. Whisk Egg Yolks:

- In a heatproof bowl, whisk the egg yolks and sugar together until the mixture is pale and slightly thick.

4. Make Coffee Mixture:

- Gradually add the cooled brewed coffee to the egg yolk mixture, whisking continuously.

5. Heat on Double Boiler:

- Place the bowl over a pot of simmering water (double boiler) and continue whisking the mixture until it thickens slightly. This step helps to cook the egg yolks and create a smooth texture. Remove from heat.

6. Add Irish Whiskey:

- Stir in the Irish whiskey while the coffee mixture is still warm. Allow it to cool to room temperature.

7. Whip the Cream:

- In a separate bowl, whip the heavy cream until stiff peaks form.

8. Combine and Fold:

- Gently fold the whipped cream into the coffee mixture until well combined. Be careful not to deflate the whipped cream.

9. Chill:

- Divide the Irish Coffee Mousse mixture into serving glasses or bowls. Cover and refrigerate for at least 2-3 hours or until set.

10. Garnish:

- Before serving, you can garnish the top of each mousse with a dusting of cocoa powder or chocolate shavings.

11. Enjoy:

- Serve chilled and enjoy this light and flavorful Irish Coffee Mousse.

Irish Coffee Mousse is a sophisticated dessert with a perfect balance of coffee and whiskey flavors. It's an elegant finish to a meal or a delightful treat for coffee lovers.

Porter Cake:

Ingredients:

- 1 1/2 cups mixed dried fruit (raisins, sultanas, currants)
- 1/2 cup candied peel (mixed citrus peel)
- 1 1/4 cups strong black tea
- 1/2 cup unsalted butter, softened
- 1 cup brown sugar
- 2 large eggs, beaten
- 2 cups all-purpose flour
- 1 teaspoon baking powder
- 1/2 teaspoon ground mixed spice (or pumpkin pie spice)
- 1/2 teaspoon ground cinnamon
- 1/2 cup porter or stout beer (such as Guinness)
- 1 tablespoon black treacle or molasses

Instructions:

1. Prepare the Fruit Mixture:

- Place the mixed dried fruit and candied peel in a bowl. Pour the hot black tea over the fruit mixture and let it soak overnight, allowing the fruit to absorb the tea.

2. Preheat the Oven:

- Preheat your oven to 325°F (160°C). Grease and line a 9-inch (23 cm) round cake tin with parchment paper.

3. Cream Butter and Sugar:

- In a large mixing bowl, cream together the softened butter and brown sugar until light and fluffy.

4. Add Eggs:

- Gradually add the beaten eggs to the butter and sugar mixture, beating well after each addition.

5. Sift Dry Ingredients:

- In a separate bowl, sift together the flour, baking powder, ground mixed spice, and ground cinnamon.

6. Combine Wet and Dry Ingredients:

- Add the dry ingredients to the creamed mixture in batches, alternating with the porter or stout beer. Mix well after each addition.

7. Add Fruit Mixture:

- Stir in the soaked fruit mixture, along with any remaining tea that was not absorbed by the fruit.

8. Add Treacle:

- Mix in the black treacle or molasses until well combined.

9. Pour into Cake Tin:

- Pour the batter into the prepared cake tin, smoothing the top with a spatula.

10. Bake:

- Bake in the preheated oven for approximately 1 hour and 30 minutes to 1 hour and 45 minutes, or until a skewer inserted into the center comes out clean.

11. Cool:

- Allow the cake to cool in the tin for about 10 minutes, then transfer it to a wire rack to cool completely.

12. Enjoy:

- Once cooled, slice and enjoy the rich and flavorful Porter Cake.

Porter Cake is often enjoyed during holidays or special occasions in Ireland. The addition of porter or stout beer gives the cake a unique depth of flavor, and the combination of spices and dried fruits makes it a festive and comforting treat.

Barmbrack (Irish Tea Bread):

Ingredients:

- 2 cups mixed dried fruit (raisins, sultanas, currants)
- 1 1/2 cups hot black tea
- 3 cups all-purpose flour
- 1 cup brown sugar
- 1 teaspoon mixed spice (or pumpkin pie spice)
- 1/2 teaspoon ground cinnamon
- 1 large egg, beaten
- 1 tablespoon black treacle or molasses
- 1 teaspoon baking powder

Instructions:

1. Soak the Dried Fruit:

- Place the mixed dried fruit in a bowl and pour hot black tea over it. Allow it to soak for at least a few hours or preferably overnight, allowing the fruit to plump up and absorb the tea.

2. Preheat the Oven:

- Preheat your oven to 350°F (180°C). Grease and line a loaf pan with parchment paper.

3. Prepare the Batter:

- In a large mixing bowl, sift together the flour, brown sugar, mixed spice, cinnamon, and baking powder.

- Add the beaten egg, soaked dried fruit (including any remaining tea not absorbed), and black treacle or molasses to the dry ingredients. Mix well to combine.

4. Pour into Loaf Pan:

    - Pour the batter into the prepared loaf pan, smoothing the top with a spatula.

5. Bake:

    - Bake in the preheated oven for approximately 1 hour or until a skewer inserted into the center comes out clean.

6. Cool:

    - Allow the Barmbrack to cool in the pan for about 10 minutes, then transfer it to a wire rack to cool completely.

7. Serve:

    - Slice and serve the Barmbrack on its own or with a spread of butter. It's delicious with a cup of tea.

8. Enjoy:

    - Enjoy this traditional Irish Tea Bread, filled with plump, soaked fruit and warm spices.

Barmbrack is often associated with Halloween in Ireland, where small trinkets or charms are sometimes baked into the bread to predict the future for those who find them. However, it's a delightful treat that can be enjoyed throughout the year. The soaked fruit adds moisture and a burst of flavor, making it a comforting and satisfying bread.

Irish Cream Profiteroles:

Ingredients:

For the Choux Pastry:

- 1 cup water
- 1/2 cup unsalted butter
- 1 cup all-purpose flour
- 4 large eggs

For the Irish Cream Filling:

- 1 cup heavy cream
- 3 tablespoons confectioners' sugar (powdered sugar)
- 2 tablespoons Irish cream liqueur (such as Baileys)

For the Chocolate Sauce:

- 1/2 cup semi-sweet chocolate chips
- 1/4 cup heavy cream
- 1 tablespoon Irish cream liqueur

Instructions:

1. Prepare the Choux Pastry:

- Preheat your oven to 400°F (200°C). Line a baking sheet with parchment paper.
- In a saucepan, combine water and butter and bring to a boil. Once boiling, remove from heat and quickly stir in the flour until a smooth dough forms.
- Let the dough cool for a few minutes. Add eggs one at a time, beating well after each addition, until the dough is smooth and glossy.
- Transfer the choux pastry to a piping bag fitted with a large round tip. Pipe small mounds (about 1.5 inches in diameter) onto the prepared baking sheet.
- Bake in the preheated oven for 15-20 minutes or until the profiteroles are golden brown and puffed up. Allow them to cool completely.

2. Prepare the Irish Cream Filling:

- In a bowl, whip the heavy cream and confectioners' sugar until stiff peaks form.
- Gently fold in the Irish cream liqueur until well combined.

3. Fill the Profiteroles:

- Cut the cooled profiteroles in half horizontally. Spoon or pipe the Irish cream filling into the bottom halves and replace the tops.

4. Make the Chocolate Sauce:

- In a small saucepan or using a microwave, heat the chocolate chips and heavy cream until the chocolate is melted and smooth. Stir in the Irish cream liqueur.

5. Drizzle with Chocolate Sauce:

- Drizzle the chocolate sauce over the filled profiteroles.

6. Serve:

- Serve the Irish Cream Profiteroles immediately, or refrigerate until ready to serve.

7. Enjoy:

- Enjoy these delicious and elegant Irish Cream Profiteroles as a decadent dessert.

Irish Cream Profiteroles are a delightful way to incorporate the rich and creamy flavor of Irish cream into a classic French pastry. The combination of light choux pastry, luscious filling, and chocolate sauce makes this dessert a perfect treat for special occasions or as a sweet indulgence.

Breads:

Traditional Irish Soda Bread:

Ingredients:

- 4 cups all-purpose flour
- 1 teaspoon baking soda (bicarbonate of soda)
- 1 teaspoon salt
- 1 and 3/4 cups buttermilk

Instructions:

1. Preheat the Oven:

   - Preheat your oven to 425°F (220°C). Dust a baking sheet with a little flour.

2. Mix Dry Ingredients:

   - In a large mixing bowl, combine the all-purpose flour, baking soda, and salt.

3. Create a Well:

   - Make a well in the center of the flour mixture.

4. Add Buttermilk:

   - Pour most of the buttermilk into the well. Reserve a small amount for brushing the top.

5. Mix Gently:

   - Using a wooden spoon or your hands, gently stir the flour into the buttermilk until you have a soft, sticky dough. Be cautious not to overmix.

6. Knead Briefly:

    - Turn the dough onto a floured surface and lightly knead it a couple of times, just enough to bring it together.

7. Shape the Dough:

    - Form the dough into a round about 1.5 to 2 inches thick.

8. Score the Dough:

    - Use a sharp knife to make a deep cross on top of the dough. This helps the bread to expand as it bakes.

9. Brush with Buttermilk:

    - Brush the top of the dough with the reserved buttermilk.

10. Bake:

    - Place the dough on the prepared baking sheet and bake in the preheated oven for about 15 minutes. Then reduce the oven temperature to 400°F (200°C) and continue baking for another 20-30 minutes, or until the bread is golden brown and sounds hollow when tapped on the bottom.

11. Cool:

    - Allow the Irish Soda Bread to cool on a wire rack.

12. Enjoy:

    - Slice and enjoy the traditional Irish Soda Bread, preferably with butter and a cup of tea.

Tips:

- If you don't have buttermilk, you can make a substitute by adding 1 tablespoon of white vinegar or lemon juice to a measuring cup and filling it with milk until you reach the 1 and 3/4 cup mark. Let it sit for 5-10 minutes before using.
- Some variations of Irish Soda Bread include adding a handful of raisins or currants to the dry ingredients for a sweeter version known as "Spotted Dog."

This straightforward recipe captures the essence of traditional Irish Soda Bread – a crusty exterior and a soft, slightly dense interior. It's perfect for serving alongside a hearty Irish stew or enjoyed on its own.

Brown Soda Bread:

Ingredients:

- 2 cups wholemeal (whole wheat) flour
- 2 cups all-purpose flour
- 1 teaspoon baking soda (bicarbonate of soda)
- 1 teaspoon salt
- 1 and 3/4 cups buttermilk

Instructions:

1. Preheat the Oven:

- Preheat your oven to 425°F (220°C). Dust a baking sheet with a little flour.

2. Mix Dry Ingredients:

- In a large mixing bowl, combine the wholemeal flour, all-purpose flour, baking soda, and salt.

3. Create a Well:

- Make a well in the center of the flour mixture.

4. Add Buttermilk:

- Pour most of the buttermilk into the well. Reserve a small amount for brushing the top.

5. Mix Gently:

- Using a wooden spoon or your hands, gently stir the flour into the buttermilk until you have a soft, sticky dough. Be cautious not to overmix.

6. Knead Briefly:

- Turn the dough onto a floured surface and lightly knead it a couple of times, just enough to bring it together.

7. Shape the Dough:

- Form the dough into a round about 1.5 to 2 inches thick.

8. Score the Dough:

- Use a sharp knife to make a deep cross on top of the dough. This helps the bread to expand as it bakes.

9. Brush with Buttermilk:

- Brush the top of the dough with the reserved buttermilk.

10. Bake:

- Place the dough on the prepared baking sheet and bake in the preheated oven for about 15 minutes. Then reduce the oven temperature to 400°F (200°C) and continue baking for another 20-30 minutes, or until the bread is golden brown and sounds hollow when tapped on the bottom.

11. Cool:

- Allow the Brown Soda Bread to cool on a wire rack.

12. Enjoy:

- Slice and enjoy the hearty and nutritious Brown Soda Bread, perhaps with butter or your favorite toppings.

This Brown Soda Bread recipe maintains the simplicity and quick preparation associated with traditional Irish Soda Bread while incorporating the wholesome goodness of wholemeal flour. It's a versatile bread that pairs well with various spreads, cheeses, or as an accompaniment to soups and stews.

Wheaten Bread:

Ingredients:

- 2 cups whole wheat flour
- 1 cup all-purpose flour
- 1 teaspoon baking soda (bicarbonate of soda)
- 1/2 teaspoon salt
- 1 tablespoon honey or molasses
- 1 and 3/4 cups buttermilk

Instructions:

1. Preheat the Oven:

    - Preheat your oven to 425°F (220°C). Dust a baking sheet with a little flour.

2. Mix Dry Ingredients:

    - In a large mixing bowl, combine the whole wheat flour, all-purpose flour, baking soda, and salt.

3. Add Sweetener:

    - Add the honey or molasses to the dry ingredients and mix well.

4. Create a Well:

    - Make a well in the center of the flour mixture.

5. Add Buttermilk:

    - Pour most of the buttermilk into the well. Reserve a small amount for brushing the top.

6. Mix Gently:

    - Using a wooden spoon or your hands, gently stir the flour into the buttermilk until you have a soft, sticky dough. Be cautious not to overmix.

7. Knead Briefly:

- Turn the dough onto a floured surface and lightly knead it a couple of times, just enough to bring it together.

8. Shape the Dough:

- Form the dough into a round about 1.5 to 2 inches thick.

9. Score the Dough:

- Use a sharp knife to make a deep cross on top of the dough. This helps the bread to expand as it bakes.

10. Brush with Buttermilk:

- Brush the top of the dough with the reserved buttermilk.

11. Bake:

- Place the dough on the prepared baking sheet and bake in the preheated oven for about 15 minutes. Then reduce the oven temperature to 400°F (200°C) and continue baking for another 20-30 minutes, or until the bread is golden brown and sounds hollow when tapped on the bottom.

12. Cool:

- Allow the Wheaten Bread to cool on a wire rack.

13. Enjoy:

- Slice and enjoy this hearty and wholesome Wheaten Bread with your favorite toppings.

Wheaten Bread is a popular choice in Irish homes, and its nutty flavor and dense texture make it a delightful addition to meals. Whether served with butter and jam for breakfast or alongside soups and stews for dinner, Wheaten Bread is a versatile and tasty treat.

Potato Farls:

Ingredients:

- 2 cups mashed potatoes (cooled)
- 1 cup all-purpose flour, plus extra for dusting
- Salt, to taste
- Butter or oil for frying

Instructions:

1. Prepare Mashed Potatoes:

- Make mashed potatoes by boiling peeled and diced potatoes until tender. Mash the potatoes and let them cool.

2. Mix Mashed Potatoes and Flour:

- In a large bowl, combine the mashed potatoes and flour. Add a pinch of salt to taste.

3. Form a Dough:

- Mix the ingredients until they come together to form a dough. The mixture should be firm but pliable. If it's too sticky, add a bit more flour.

4. Roll Out the Dough:

- On a floured surface, roll out the dough into a round about 1/4 to 1/2 inch thick.

5. Cut into Farls:

- Using a knife, cut the rolled-out dough into quarters, creating four equal farls.

6. Heat the Pan:

- Heat a griddle or a non-stick frying pan over medium heat. Add a little butter or oil to prevent sticking.

7. Cook the Farls:

- Place the farls in the pan and cook for about 5-7 minutes on each side, or until they are golden brown and cooked through.

8. Serve:

- Once cooked, remove the farls from the pan and serve them hot.

9. Enjoy:

- Enjoy the Potato Farls on their own, with butter, or as part of a traditional Irish breakfast.

Optional Tips:

- You can customize the flavor by adding chopped herbs, grated cheese, or even a touch of garlic to the mashed potatoes before mixing them with flour.
- Potato Farls are often served with a traditional Irish breakfast alongside items like eggs, bacon, sausage, and black and white pudding.

Potato Farls are a beloved part of Irish cuisine and make for a delicious and satisfying dish. Whether enjoyed for breakfast or as a side, their simplicity and versatility make them a staple in many Irish households.

Irish Barmbrack Bread:

Ingredients:

- 2 cups mixed dried fruit (raisins, sultanas, currants)
- 1 cup hot black tea
- 1/2 cup brown sugar
- 1 large egg, beaten
- 4 cups all-purpose flour
- 1 teaspoon mixed spice (or pumpkin pie spice)
- 1/2 teaspoon ground cinnamon
- 1/4 teaspoon ground nutmeg
- Pinch of salt
- 1 packet (7g) active dry yeast
- 1/4 cup butter, melted

Instructions:

1. Prepare Dried Fruit:

- Place the mixed dried fruit in a bowl and pour hot black tea over it. Let it soak for at least a few hours or preferably overnight, allowing the fruit to plump up and absorb the tea.

2. Activate Yeast:

- In a small bowl, dissolve the yeast in a little warm water (about 1/4 cup) with a pinch of sugar. Let it sit for 5-10 minutes until frothy.

3. Mix Dry Ingredients:

- In a large mixing bowl, combine the flour, brown sugar, mixed spice, ground cinnamon, ground nutmeg, and a pinch of salt.

4. Create a Well:

- Make a well in the center of the dry ingredients.

5. Combine Wet Ingredients:

- Add the beaten egg, melted butter, activated yeast mixture, and the soaked dried fruit (including any remaining tea not absorbed) to the well. Mix everything together until you have a soft dough.

6. Knead Dough:

- Turn the dough out onto a floured surface and knead it for about 10 minutes until it becomes smooth and elastic.

7. Let it Rise:

- Place the dough in a lightly oiled bowl, cover it with a clean kitchen towel, and let it rise in a warm place for about 1-2 hours or until doubled in size.

8. Shape the Bread:

- Punch down the risen dough and shape it into a round loaf. Place it on a baking sheet lined with parchment paper.

9. Preheat Oven:

- Preheat your oven to 350°F (180°C).

10. Let it Rise Again:

- Cover the shaped loaf with a kitchen towel and let it rise for another 30 minutes.

11. Bake:

    - Bake the Barmbrack in the preheated oven for approximately 40-50 minutes or until the bread is golden brown and sounds hollow when tapped on the bottom.

12. Cool:

    - Allow the Barmbrack to cool on a wire rack before slicing.

13. Enjoy:

    - Slice and enjoy the deliciously spiced and fruit-filled Irish Barmbrack, preferably with a spread of butter.

Barmbrack is often associated with Halloween in Ireland, and it's a traditional practice to include small trinkets or charms in the bread, each with a specific meaning for the person who finds it. The dried fruit and spices give the bread a rich, flavorful taste.

Breakfast:

Irish Breakfast Fry-Up:

Ingredients:

- Irish sausages
- Irish bacon (rashers)
- Black pudding
- White pudding
- Eggs
- Tomatoes
- Mushrooms
- Baked beans
- Irish soda bread or toast
- Butter for cooking
- Salt and pepper to taste

Instructions:

1. Cook the Sausages:

   - In a frying pan, cook the Irish sausages according to the package instructions until they are browned and cooked through.

2. Fry the Bacon:

   - In the same pan or a separate one, fry the Irish bacon rashers until they are crispy. Remove excess fat if desired.

3. Prepare Black and White Pudding:

   - Slice the black pudding and white pudding into rounds. Fry them in the pan until they are browned on both sides.

4. Cook Eggs:

   - In the same pan, fry or poach the eggs to your liking.

5. Grill Tomatoes and Sauté Mushrooms:

- Grill halved tomatoes until they are slightly softened. In a separate pan, sauté sliced mushrooms in butter until they are cooked through.

6. Heat Baked Beans:

- Heat the baked beans in a saucepan or microwave.

7. Toast Irish Soda Bread or Bread:

- Toast slices of Irish soda bread or your preferred bread.

8. Assemble the Fry-Up:

- Arrange the cooked sausages, bacon, black pudding, white pudding, eggs, grilled tomatoes, sautéed mushrooms, and toasted bread on a plate.

9. Serve with Baked Beans:

- Place a portion of heated baked beans on the plate.

10. Garnish and Season:

- Garnish with a sprinkle of salt and pepper, and add a pat of butter to the toast if desired.

11. Enjoy:

- Serve the Irish Breakfast Fry-Up hot and enjoy a hearty and satisfying meal.

Tips:

- Feel free to customize the breakfast with additional items such as hash browns, grilled sautéed spinach, or fried potatoes.
- Accompany the breakfast with a cup of strong Irish tea or coffee.

This Irish Breakfast Fry-Up is a delicious and hearty way to start the day, featuring a variety of savory elements that reflect the traditional flavors of Irish cuisine.

Boxty Breakfast Tacos:

Ingredients:

For the Boxty:

- 2 cups grated raw potatoes
- 1 cup mashed potatoes
- 1 cup all-purpose flour
- 1 cup buttermilk
- 1 teaspoon baking powder
- Salt and pepper to taste
- Butter or oil for cooking

For the Breakfast Tacos:

- Eggs (scrambled or fried)
- Cooked Irish bacon or regular bacon
- Grated cheese (cheddar or your choice)
- Salsa or pico de gallo
- Avocado slices
- Fresh cilantro, chopped (optional)
- Salt and pepper to taste

Instructions:

1. Prepare the Boxty:

    Grate raw potatoes and squeeze out excess moisture.
    In a large bowl, combine the grated potatoes, mashed potatoes, flour, baking powder, buttermilk, salt, and pepper. Mix until well combined.
    Heat a skillet or griddle over medium heat and add butter or oil.
    Spoon portions of the boxty batter onto the hot surface and spread them into thin pancakes. Cook until golden brown on both sides.

2. Cook the Eggs and Bacon:

    In a separate pan, cook scrambled or fried eggs to your liking.
    Cook Irish bacon or regular bacon until crispy.

3. Assemble the Tacos:

> Place a boxty pancake on a plate.
> Layer with scrambled or fried eggs, cooked bacon, grated cheese, salsa or pico de gallo, and avocado slices.
> Sprinkle with chopped cilantro (if using), and season with salt and pepper to taste.

4. Serve:

- Serve the Boxty Breakfast Tacos immediately while the boxty is warm and the toppings are fresh.

5. Enjoy:

- Enjoy the fusion of Irish and Mexican flavors in this creative and delicious breakfast dish.

Feel free to customize the toppings to suit your taste. These Boxty Breakfast Tacos offer a unique twist on traditional Irish boxty, combining it with the bold and flavorful elements of breakfast tacos.

Black Pudding and Apple Pancakes:

Ingredients:

For the Pancakes:

- 1 cup all-purpose flour
- 1 tablespoon sugar
- 1 teaspoon baking powder
- 1/2 teaspoon baking soda
- 1/4 teaspoon salt
- 3/4 cup buttermilk
- 1 large egg
- 2 tablespoons unsalted butter, melted
- Butter or oil for cooking

For the Black Pudding and Apple Topping:

- 1/2 lb (about 225g) black pudding, sliced
- 1-2 apples, cored and thinly sliced
- 1 tablespoon butter
- 1 tablespoon brown sugar
- 1/2 teaspoon ground cinnamon (optional)
- Maple syrup for serving

Instructions:

1. Prepare the Pancake Batter:

    In a large bowl, whisk together the flour, sugar, baking powder, baking soda, and salt.
    In a separate bowl, whisk together the buttermilk, egg, and melted butter.
    Pour the wet ingredients into the dry ingredients and gently fold until just combined. Do not overmix; a few lumps are okay.

2. Cook the Pancakes:

    Heat a griddle or non-stick skillet over medium heat. Add a small amount of butter or oil.

Pour 1/4 cup of batter onto the griddle for each pancake. Cook until bubbles form on the surface, then flip and cook the other side until golden brown. Repeat until all the batter is used.

3. Prepare the Black Pudding and Apple Topping:

   In a separate pan, cook the black pudding slices over medium heat until browned on both sides. Remove from the pan and set aside.
   In the same pan, add a tablespoon of butter. Add the sliced apples and cook until they begin to soften.
   Sprinkle brown sugar over the apples and stir to coat. Cook for an additional 2-3 minutes until the apples are caramelized. Add ground cinnamon if using.

4. Assemble the Pancakes:

   Place a pancake on a plate.
   Top with slices of cooked black pudding and the caramelized apple mixture.
   Repeat the process, creating a stack of pancakes with layers of black pudding and apples.

5. Serve:

   - Drizzle maple syrup over the top of the pancake stack.

6. Enjoy:

   - Enjoy the unique and delicious flavors of Black Pudding and Apple Pancakes!

This dish combines the savory richness of black pudding with the sweetness of caramelized apples, creating a delightful and flavorful pancake stack. The maple syrup adds a touch of sweetness that complements the savory components.

Porridge with Honey and Whiskey:

Ingredients:

- 1 cup rolled oats
- 2 cups milk (dairy or plant-based)
- Pinch of salt
- 1-2 tablespoons honey (adjust to taste)
- 1-2 tablespoons Irish whiskey (adjust to taste)
- Optional toppings: sliced bananas, berries, or chopped nuts

Instructions:

1. Cook the Porridge:

    In a saucepan, combine the rolled oats, milk, and a pinch of salt.
    Bring the mixture to a gentle simmer over medium heat, stirring occasionally.

2. Simmer and Stir:

    Reduce the heat to low and simmer the porridge until it reaches your desired consistency, usually about 5-7 minutes.
    Stir frequently to prevent the oats from sticking to the bottom of the pan.

3. Sweeten with Honey:

    Once the porridge is cooked, remove it from the heat.
    Stir in 1-2 tablespoons of honey, adjusting the sweetness to your liking.

4. Add Whiskey:

    Add 1-2 tablespoons of Irish whiskey to the porridge. Adjust the amount based on your preference for the whiskey flavor.
    Stir well to incorporate the whiskey into the porridge.

5. Serve:

    Spoon the porridge into bowls.
    Optionally, top with sliced bananas, berries, or chopped nuts.

6. Drizzle with Honey:

   Drizzle a little extra honey on top for added sweetness, if desired.

7. Enjoy:

   - Serve the Porridge with Honey and Whiskey warm, and enjoy a comforting and flavorful breakfast.

This hearty and warming porridge combines the creaminess of oats with the sweetness of honey and a hint of Irish whiskey. It's a delightful way to start your day, especially when the weather is chilly. Adjust the honey and whiskey amounts according to your taste preferences.

Irish Sausage Rolls:

Ingredients:

- 1 pound (450g) good-quality pork sausage meat (Irish or your preferred variety)
- 1 sheet of puff pastry, thawed if frozen
- 1 egg (beaten, for egg wash)
- Optional: Dijon mustard for serving

Instructions:

1. Preheat the Oven:

- Preheat your oven to 400°F (200°C).

2. Prepare the Sausage Meat:

- If the sausage meat is in casings, remove it from the casings and place it in a bowl. If you have loose sausage meat, you can skip this step.

3. Roll Out the Puff Pastry:

- Roll out the puff pastry sheet on a lightly floured surface to create a rectangle. The size will depend on the thickness of the sausage layer you desire.

4. Add Sausage Meat:

- Spread the sausage meat evenly over the puff pastry, leaving a small border along one edge.

5. Roll and Seal:

- Roll the pastry tightly over the sausage meat, sealing the edge with a bit of water. The seam should be on the bottom.

6. Cut into Rolls:

- Cut the rolled pastry and sausage into smaller rolls of your preferred size. You can make bite-sized rolls or larger ones.

7. Score the Top:

- Use a sharp knife to score the top of each roll lightly. This helps the steam escape during baking.

8. Egg Wash:

- Brush the top of each roll with beaten egg to give them a golden finish.

9. Bake:

- Place the rolls on a baking sheet and bake in the preheated oven for approximately 20-25 minutes, or until the pastry is golden brown and the sausage is cooked through.

10. Serve:

- Allow the sausage rolls to cool for a few minutes before slicing into portions. Serve them warm, optionally with Dijon mustard for dipping.

11. Enjoy:

- Enjoy the Irish Sausage Rolls as a snack, appetizer, or party treat.

These Irish Sausage Rolls are versatile and can be customized with additional seasonings, herbs, or spices to suit your taste. They are perfect for gatherings, picnics, or as a tasty addition to any meal.

Beverages:

Irish Coffee:

Ingredients:

- 1 cup hot brewed coffee
- 1 to 1.5 ounces (30 to 45 ml) Irish whiskey
- 1 to 2 teaspoons brown sugar (adjust to taste)
- Heavy cream

Instructions:

1. Prepare the Coffee:

    - Brew a cup of your favorite hot coffee. Make it strong, as the whiskey and cream will mellow the flavor.

2. Preheat the Glass:

    - Preheat a heat-resistant glass or mug by filling it with hot water. Let it sit for a moment, then discard the water.

3. Add Ingredients:

    - Pour the hot brewed coffee into the preheated glass.
    - Add the Irish whiskey to the coffee.
    - Stir in brown sugar to taste. Adjust the sweetness according to your preference.

4. Whip the Cream:

    - In a separate bowl, lightly whip the heavy cream. It should have a pourable consistency; avoid over-whipping.

5. Layer the Cream:

    - Gently pour the whipped cream over the back of a spoon to create a layer on top of the coffee. The cream should float on the surface.

6. Serve:

- Serve the Irish Coffee immediately while it's hot.

7. Enjoy:

- Sip and enjoy the rich and comforting flavors of Irish Coffee.

Tips:

- Experiment with different types of Irish whiskey to find your preferred flavor profile.
- You can use a spoon to help float the cream on top of the coffee, or you can gently pour it over the back of the spoon.

Irish Coffee is a delightful blend of flavors – the boldness of coffee, the warmth of Irish whiskey, the sweetness of brown sugar, and the richness of cream. It's a classic cocktail that has stood the test of time and is enjoyed by many.

Black Velvet Cocktail:

Ingredients:

- 1/2 glass stout beer (such as Guinness)
- 1/2 glass champagne or sparkling wine (chilled)

Instructions:

1. Choose the Glass:

- Use a champagne flute or any tall, narrow glass for a visually appealing presentation.

2. Pour the Stout:

- Fill half of the glass with stout beer. You can use a spoon to gently pour it over the back of the spoon to minimize foam.

3. Add the Champagne:

- Carefully pour the champagne or sparkling wine over the back of a spoon to create a layer on top of the stout. The two layers should remain separate.

4. Serve:

- Serve the Black Velvet cocktail immediately, while it's visually striking with its distinctive layers.

5. Enjoy:

- Sip and enjoy the unique combination of the rich, dark beer with the light and effervescent champagne.

Tips:

- Use chilled champagne or sparkling wine for a refreshing touch.
- Experiment with different types of stout beer to vary the flavor profile of the cocktail.

The Black Velvet cocktail is named for its visually striking appearance, resembling the texture of the fabric it's named after. It's a sophisticated drink that plays on the contrast between the dark beer and the bubbly champagne, creating a delightful and surprising combination of flavors and textures.

Hot Whiskey:

Ingredients:

- 2 oz (60 ml) Irish whiskey
- 1 tablespoon honey (adjust to taste)
- 1/2 lemon, juiced
- Hot water (about 6-8 oz or 180-240 ml)
- Optional: Lemon slice and/or cinnamon stick for garnish

Instructions:

1. Heat the Mug:

   - Start by preheating your mug or heat-resistant glass by filling it with hot water. Let it sit for a moment, then discard the water.

2. Add Ingredients:

   - Pour the Irish whiskey into the preheated mug.
   - Add honey and fresh lemon juice to the whiskey.

3. Fill with Hot Water:

   - Fill the mug with hot water, leaving some space at the top for stirring.

4. Stir Well:

   - Stir the ingredients thoroughly to ensure the honey is dissolved and the flavors are well combined.

5. Optional Garnish:

   - If desired, garnish with a lemon slice and/or a cinnamon stick.

6. Enjoy:

   - Sip and enjoy the comforting warmth of Hot Whiskey.

Tips:

- Adjust the honey to your preferred level of sweetness.
- You can use a different type of whiskey if you prefer a particular flavor profile.

Hot Whiskey is not only a soothing drink, but it's also believed to have some medicinal properties, making it a go-to for colds or sore throats. The combination of whiskey, honey, and lemon creates a comforting and flavorful beverage that's sure to warm you up from the inside.

Irish Cream Liqueur:

Ingredients:

- 1 cup Irish whiskey
- 1 cup heavy cream
- 1 can (14 ounces) sweetened condensed milk
- 2 tablespoons chocolate syrup
- 1 teaspoon instant coffee granules
- 1 teaspoon vanilla extract
- 1/2 teaspoon almond extract (optional)

Instructions:

1. Combine Ingredients:

   - In a blender, combine the Irish whiskey, heavy cream, sweetened condensed milk, chocolate syrup, instant coffee granules, vanilla extract, and almond extract if using.

2. Blend:

   - Blend the ingredients on high speed until well combined and smooth.

3. Taste and Adjust:

   - Taste the mixture and adjust the sweetness or thickness by adding more sweetened condensed milk if needed.

4. Store:

   - Pour the Irish Cream Liqueur into a clean and airtight bottle or jar.

5. Refrigerate:

   - Refrigerate the liqueur for at least a couple of hours or overnight to allow the flavors to meld and the mixture to chill.

6. Shake Before Serving:

- Shake the bottle well before serving to ensure the ingredients are well mixed.

7. Enjoy:

- Serve the Irish Cream Liqueur over ice, in coffee, or use it as an ingredient in cocktails or desserts.

Tips:

- Experiment with the flavor by adjusting the chocolate syrup, coffee, or extracts to suit your taste.
- You can add a touch of cinnamon or nutmeg for extra warmth and flavor.

Homemade Irish Cream Liqueur makes for a delightful and personalized beverage. It's perfect for sipping on its own, adding to coffee, or using as an ingredient in cocktails and desserts. Be sure to store it in the refrigerator, and shake well before each use.

Dingle Gin and Tonic:

Ingredients:

- 2 oz (60 ml) Dingle Gin
- Tonic water (high-quality tonic water works best)
- Ice cubes
- Garnish: Slice of grapefruit or a wedge of lime

Instructions:

1. Chill the Glass:

   - Place a highball or balloon glass in the freezer or fill it with ice water to chill while you prepare the other ingredients.

2. Fill the Glass with Ice:

   - Add ice cubes to the chilled glass. The quality of the ice can enhance the overall drink, so consider using large, clear ice cubes.

3. Pour the Dingle Gin:

   - Measure 2 ounces (60 ml) of Dingle Gin and pour it over the ice in the glass.

4. Top with Tonic Water:

   - Top up the glass with your favorite tonic water. Use a good-quality tonic water that complements the botanicals in the gin.

5. Gently Stir:

   - Use a bar spoon or a stirring stick to gently stir the gin and tonic mixture. This helps to incorporate the flavors without losing the effervescence of the tonic water.

6. Garnish:

   - Garnish the drink with a slice of grapefruit or a wedge of lime. This adds a citrusy aroma that complements the botanicals in the gin.

7. Enjoy:

- Sip and enjoy the crisp and refreshing Dingle Gin and Tonic.

Tips:

- Experiment with different garnishes like a sprig of fresh rosemary, cucumber slices, or a few juniper berries for added aromatic complexity.
- Consider using a flavored tonic water for an extra layer of taste.

The Dingle Gin and Tonic is a simple yet sophisticated cocktail that allows the unique botanicals of Dingle Gin to shine. Adjust the gin-to-tonic ratio and garnishes according to your taste preferences for a personalized and enjoyable drink.

Redbreast Irish Whiskey Sour:

Ingredients:

- 2 oz (60 ml) Redbreast Irish Whiskey
- 3/4 oz (22.5 ml) simple syrup (equal parts water and sugar, dissolved)
- 3/4 oz (22.5 ml) fresh lemon juice
- Ice cubes
- Lemon slice or cherry for garnish (optional)

Instructions:

1. Prepare Simple Syrup:

   - In a small saucepan, combine equal parts water and sugar. Heat over low heat, stirring until the sugar dissolves. Allow it to cool before using.

2. Chill the Glass:

   - Place a rocks glass in the freezer or fill it with ice water to chill while you prepare the cocktail.

3. Combine Ingredients:

   - In a shaker, add Redbreast Irish Whiskey, simple syrup, and fresh lemon juice.

4. Add Ice and Shake:

   - Fill the shaker with ice cubes, then shake the mixture vigorously for about 10-15 seconds to chill the ingredients.

5. Strain Into Glass:

   - Discard the ice from the chilled rocks glass. Strain the shaken mixture into the glass over fresh ice.

6. Garnish:

   - Garnish the Redbreast Irish Whiskey Sour with a lemon slice or a cherry if desired.

7. Enjoy:

    - Sip and savor the deliciously balanced flavors of the Redbreast Irish Whiskey Sour.

Tips:

- Adjust the sweetness by adding more or less simple syrup according to your taste.
- You can experiment with different garnishes, such as an orange twist or a few drops of bitters.

The Redbreast Irish Whiskey Sour is a smooth and sophisticated cocktail that showcases the distinct qualities of Redbreast Irish Whiskey. The combination of whiskey, citrus, and sweetness creates a well-balanced and refreshing drink.

Poitín Punch:

Ingredients:

- 1 1/2 oz (45 ml) poitín
- 1 oz (30 ml) orange juice
- 1 oz (30 ml) pineapple juice
- 1/2 oz (15 ml) grenadine syrup
- Ice cubes
- Orange slice or cherry for garnish

Instructions:

1. Chill the Glass:

    - Place a highball glass in the freezer or fill it with ice water to chill while you prepare the cocktail.

2. Combine Ingredients:

    - In a shaker, add poitín, orange juice, pineapple juice, and grenadine syrup.

3. Add Ice and Shake:

    - Fill the shaker with ice cubes, then shake the mixture well to chill the ingredients.

4. Strain Into Glass:

    - Discard the ice from the chilled highball glass. Strain the shaken mixture into the glass over fresh ice.

5. Garnish:

    - Garnish the Poitín Punch with an orange slice or a cherry.

6. Enjoy:

    - Sip and experience the unique and bold flavors of Poitín Punch.

Tips:

- Poitín is a strong spirit, so consume this punch responsibly.
- Adjust the sweetness by adding more or less grenadine syrup according to your taste.

The Poitín Punch is a bold and fruity cocktail that highlights the distinctive characteristics of poitín. Its high-proof nature makes it a potent beverage, so it's essential to enjoy it responsibly. Feel free to experiment with the juice ratios to find the balance that suits your palate.

Irish Stout Float:

Ingredients:

- 1 can or bottle (12 oz) of Irish stout beer (e.g., Guinness)
- 2-3 scoops of vanilla ice cream

Instructions:

1. Chill the Glasses:

   - Place the glasses in the freezer or fill them with ice water to chill while you prepare the other ingredients.

2. Scoop Vanilla Ice Cream:

   - Scoop 2-3 generous scoops of vanilla ice cream and set them aside.

3. Open the Irish Stout:

   - Open the can or bottle of Irish stout beer. Allow it to settle for a moment if it's fizzy.

4. Assemble the Float:

   - Carefully pour the Irish stout over the scoops of vanilla ice cream in the chilled glasses. The beer will create a frothy head as it meets the cold ice cream.

5. Serve Immediately:

   - Serve the Irish Stout Float immediately while it's visually appealing with the foamy head and creamy ice cream.

6. Enjoy:

   - Use a spoon or a straw to enjoy sips of the creamy float along with the effervescence of the Irish stout.

Tips:

- Experiment with different flavors of ice cream, such as chocolate or caramel, to complement the stout.
- For an extra kick, you can drizzle a bit of Irish whiskey over the ice cream before pouring the stout.

The Irish Stout Float is a fun and indulgent treat that brings together the bold flavors of Irish stout and the sweetness of vanilla ice cream. It's a delightful dessert-style drink that's perfect for St. Patrick's Day or any occasion where you want to enjoy a unique and flavorful treat.

Irish Breakfast Tea Punch:

Ingredients:

- 4 cups strong brewed Irish Breakfast tea, chilled
- 1 cup orange juice
- 1/2 cup pineapple juice
- 1/4 cup lemon juice
- 1/4 cup simple syrup (equal parts water and sugar, dissolved)
- Ice cubes
- Orange slices and mint leaves for garnish (optional)

Instructions:

1. Brew Irish Breakfast Tea:

  - Brew a pot of strong Irish Breakfast tea. Allow it to steep according to the recommended time on the tea packaging. Once brewed, let it cool to room temperature and then refrigerate until chilled.

2. Prepare Simple Syrup:

  - In a small saucepan, combine equal parts water and sugar. Heat over low heat, stirring until the sugar dissolves. Allow it to cool before using.

3. Mix Ingredients:

  - In a large pitcher, combine the chilled brewed Irish Breakfast tea, orange juice, pineapple juice, lemon juice, and simple syrup. Stir well to ensure all ingredients are mixed.

4. Chill:

  - Place the pitcher in the refrigerator to chill for at least 1-2 hours, allowing the flavors to meld.

5. Serve:

  - Fill glasses with ice cubes and pour the Irish Breakfast Tea Punch over the ice.

6. Garnish:

- Garnish with orange slices and mint leaves if desired.

7. Stir Before Serving:

- Give the punch a gentle stir before serving to ensure that all the flavors are well-distributed.

8. Enjoy:

- Sip and enjoy the refreshing and citrusy flavors of the Irish Breakfast Tea Punch.

Tips:

- Adjust the sweetness by adding more or less simple syrup according to your taste.
- Experiment with different fruit juices or add fresh fruit slices for additional variety.

This Irish Breakfast Tea Punch is a delightful and thirst-quenching option for brunches, gatherings, or as a refreshing beverage on a warm day. The combination of bold Irish Breakfast tea and citrus juices creates a harmonious and invigorating punch.

Celtic Honey Mead:

Ingredients:

- 3 lbs (about 1.4 kg) honey (choose a high-quality, flavorful honey)
- 1 gallon (about 3.8 liters) water
- 1 packet of wine yeast (suitable for mead, follow the package instructions)
- Optional: 1-2 teaspoons of yeast nutrient (available at brewing supply stores)
- Optional: Additional flavorings like fruits or spices

Instructions:

1. Sanitize Equipment:

    - Thoroughly clean and sanitize all your brewing equipment, including the fermentation vessel, airlock, and stirring utensils.

2. Prepare Honey-Water Mixture:

    - In a large pot, heat about a gallon of water until warm. Add the honey to the warm water and stir until completely dissolved. This mixture is known as "must."

3. Cool the Must:

    - Allow the honey-water mixture to cool to room temperature.

4. Transfer to Fermentation Vessel:

    - Transfer the cooled must to a fermentation vessel, leaving some space at the top for foaming during fermentation.

5. Add Yeast:

    - Sprinkle the wine yeast over the must. If using yeast nutrient, add it at this stage. Stir well to ensure even distribution.

6. Seal and Attach Airlock:

- Seal the fermentation vessel with an airlock to allow gases to escape during fermentation. This prevents contamination while maintaining a controlled environment.

7. Fermentation:

- Place the fermentation vessel in a cool, dark place and let the mead ferment. The fermentation process can take several weeks.

8. Rack the Mead:

- After the initial fermentation slows down (usually a few weeks), you can rack the mead into a clean vessel, leaving the sediment behind. This helps clarify the mead.

9. Age the Mead:

- Allow the mead to age in a cool, dark place for several months. The longer it ages, the smoother and more refined the flavors will become.

10. Bottle:

- Once the mead is clear and has developed the desired flavor, it's ready to be bottled. Use sanitized bottles and corks or caps.

11. Enjoy:

- Allow the mead to bottle-condition for a few weeks before enjoying. Serve chilled and savor the flavors of your Celtic Honey Mead.

Tips:

- Feel free to experiment with additional flavorings like fruits or spices during fermentation for a unique twist.
- Take precautions to maintain cleanliness and sanitation throughout the brewing process.

Making Celtic Honey Mead is a rewarding experience that connects you to ancient brewing traditions. It's a beverage to be enjoyed slowly, allowing the complex flavors to unfold. Patience is key in mead-making, as it often improves with age.

Soups:

Irish Potato and Leek Soup:

Ingredients:

- 2 tablespoons butter
- 2 leeks, cleaned and sliced (white and light green parts only)
- 4 large potatoes, peeled and diced
- 1 onion, finely chopped
- 2 cloves garlic, minced
- 6 cups vegetable or chicken broth
- Salt and pepper to taste
- 1 cup milk or cream (optional)
- Fresh chives or parsley for garnish (optional)

Instructions:

1. Prep Ingredients:

- Clean and slice the leeks, peel and dice the potatoes, finely chop the onion, and mince the garlic.

2. Sauté Leeks and Onions:

- In a large soup pot, melt the butter over medium heat. Add the sliced leeks and chopped onions. Cook until softened but not browned, about 5-7 minutes.

3. Add Garlic and Potatoes:

- Add the minced garlic to the pot and cook for an additional 1-2 minutes. Then, add the diced potatoes and stir to combine.

4. Pour in Broth:

- Pour in the vegetable or chicken broth, ensuring that the potatoes are fully submerged. Bring the mixture to a boil.

5. Simmer:

- Reduce the heat to low, cover the pot, and let the soup simmer for about 15-20 minutes or until the potatoes are tender.

6. Blend Soup:

- Use an immersion blender to blend the soup until smooth. If you don't have an immersion blender, transfer the soup in batches to a blender and blend until smooth. Be cautious when blending hot liquids.

7. Season:

- Season the soup with salt and pepper to taste. If you prefer a creamier soup, you can add milk or cream at this stage.

8. Garnish and Serve:

- Ladle the soup into bowls. Garnish with fresh chives or parsley if desired.

9. Enjoy:

- Serve the Irish Potato and Leek Soup hot and enjoy its comforting flavors.

Tips:

- You can add a splash of fresh lemon juice or a dollop of sour cream as a finishing touch.

- Serve the soup with crusty Irish soda bread for a complete and satisfying meal.

This Irish Potato and Leek Soup is a classic comfort food with a creamy and flavorful base. It's simple to make and offers a taste of Irish culinary tradition.

Seafood Chowder:

Ingredients:

- 1/4 cup unsalted butter
- 1 onion, finely chopped
- 2 cloves garlic, minced
- 2 celery stalks, diced
- 2 carrots, diced
- 1/4 cup all-purpose flour
- 4 cups fish or seafood broth
- 2 cups diced potatoes
- 1 bay leaf
- 1 teaspoon dried thyme
- Salt and pepper to taste
- 1 cup heavy cream
- 1 pound mixed seafood (shrimp, scallops, fish fillets, etc.), chopped into bite-sized pieces
- 1/2 cup frozen corn kernels
- Fresh parsley, chopped, for garnish

Instructions:

1. Sauté Vegetables:

- In a large pot, melt the butter over medium heat. Add the chopped onion, minced garlic, diced celery, and diced carrots. Sauté until the vegetables are softened.

2. Add Flour:

- Sprinkle the flour over the sautéed vegetables and stir to combine. Cook for 2-3 minutes to eliminate the raw flour taste.

3. Pour in Broth:

- Gradually pour in the fish or seafood broth, stirring constantly to avoid lumps. Continue stirring until the mixture thickens.

4. Add Potatoes and Seasonings:

- Add the diced potatoes, bay leaf, dried thyme, salt, and pepper to the pot. Bring the mixture to a simmer and cook until the potatoes are tender.

5. Reduce Heat and Add Cream:

- Reduce the heat to low and pour in the heavy cream. Stir well to combine.

6. Add Seafood and Corn:

- Gently stir in the mixed seafood and frozen corn kernels. Cook for about 5-7 minutes or until the seafood is cooked through.

7. Adjust Seasoning:

- Taste the chowder and adjust the seasoning if necessary. Remove the bay leaf.

8. Serve:

- Ladle the seafood chowder into bowls. Garnish with chopped fresh parsley.

9. Enjoy:

- Serve the seafood chowder hot and enjoy the delicious combination of flavors.

Tips:

- Use a variety of seafood for a more diverse flavor profile.
- Feel free to add other seafood such as crab or clams, depending on your preference.

This seafood chowder is a hearty and comforting dish that showcases the flavors of the sea. It's perfect for a cozy dinner, especially during colder months. Serve it with crusty bread for a complete and satisfying meal

Dublin Coddle Soup

Ingredients:

- 6-8 pork sausages
- 8 slices bacon, chopped
- 1 large onion, finely chopped
- 3 cloves garlic, minced
- 4 potatoes, peeled and diced
- 2 carrots, diced
- 4 cups chicken or vegetable broth
- 1 bay leaf
- Salt and pepper to taste
- Fresh parsley, chopped, for garnish

Instructions:

1. Brown the Sausages and Bacon:

- In a large pot, brown the sausages and chopped bacon over medium heat. Once browned, remove them from the pot and set aside.

2. Sauté Onion and Garlic:

- In the same pot, sauté the chopped onion and minced garlic until softened.

3. Add Potatoes and Carrots:

- Add the diced potatoes and carrots to the pot. Stir to combine with the onions and garlic.

4. Pour in Broth:

- Pour in the chicken or vegetable broth, add the bay leaf, and bring the mixture to a simmer. Season with salt and pepper to taste.

5. Simmer:

- Allow the soup to simmer until the potatoes and carrots are tender.

6. Slice and Add Sausages:

- Slice the browned sausages into bite-sized pieces and add them back to the pot. Stir to incorporate.

7. Adjust Seasoning:

- Taste the soup and adjust the seasoning if necessary. Remove the bay leaf.

8. Serve:

- Ladle the Dublin Coddle Soup into bowls. Garnish with chopped fresh parsley.

9. Enjoy:

- Serve the soup hot and enjoy the comforting flavors of Dublin Coddle in a soup form.

Tips:

- You can add a splash of Irish stout for an extra layer of flavor.
- Serve the soup with crusty Irish soda bread or a baguette.

While Dublin Coddle is traditionally a stew, adapting its flavors into a soup offers a lighter and equally delicious option. This Dublin Coddle Soup is a hearty and warming dish, perfect for a comforting meal on a chilly day.

Irish Nettle Soup:

Ingredients:

- 4 cups young nettle leaves, washed and chopped
- 1 large onion, finely chopped
- 2 leeks, sliced (white and light green parts only)
- 2 potatoes, peeled and diced
- 1 tablespoon butter
- 6 cups vegetable or chicken broth
- Salt and pepper to taste
- 1 cup milk or cream (optional)
- Fresh chives or parsley for garnish (optional)

Instructions:

1. Handle Nettles Carefully:

- Wear gloves when handling nettles to avoid stings. Pick only the young, tender leaves from the top of the plants.

2. Sauté Vegetables:

- In a large pot, melt the butter over medium heat. Add the chopped onion, sliced leeks, and diced potatoes. Sauté until the vegetables are softened.

3. Add Nettles:

- Add the washed and chopped nettle leaves to the pot. Stir to combine with the other vegetables.

4. Pour in Broth:

- Pour in the vegetable or chicken broth, ensuring that the vegetables and nettles are fully submerged. Bring the mixture to a boil.

5. Simmer:

- Reduce the heat to low, cover the pot, and let the soup simmer for about 15-20 minutes or until the potatoes are tender.

6. Blend Soup:

- Use an immersion blender to blend the soup until smooth. If you don't have an immersion blender, transfer the soup in batches to a blender and blend until smooth. Be cautious when blending hot liquids.

7. Season:

- Season the soup with salt and pepper to taste. If you prefer a creamier soup, you can add milk or cream at this stage.

8. Garnish and Serve:

- Ladle the nettle soup into bowls. Garnish with fresh chives or parsley if desired.

9. Enjoy:

- Serve the Irish Nettle Soup hot and savor its unique and nutritious flavors.

Tips:

- You can add a squeeze of fresh lemon juice for a bright, citrusy note.
- Experiment with additional herbs or spices to customize the flavor.

Irish Nettle Soup is a traditional dish that highlights the use of foraged ingredients. Rich in nutrients, nettles bring a distinct flavor to the soup, making it a unique and wholesome addition to your repertoire of Irish-inspired recipes.

Colcannon Soup:

Ingredients:

- 4 tablespoons butter
- 1 onion, finely chopped
- 2 leeks, sliced (white and light green parts only)
- 3 cloves garlic, minced
- 4 cups potatoes, peeled and diced
- 6 cups vegetable or chicken broth
- 1 small head of cabbage, finely shredded
- 1 cup kale, chopped
- 1 cup milk or cream
- Salt and pepper to taste
- Fresh chives or green onions, chopped, for garnish

Instructions:

1. Sauté Vegetables:

- In a large pot, melt 2 tablespoons of butter over medium heat. Add the chopped onion, sliced leeks, and minced garlic. Sauté until the vegetables are softened.

2. Add Potatoes:

- Add the diced potatoes to the pot and stir to combine with the sautéed vegetables.

3. Pour in Broth:

- Pour in the vegetable or chicken broth, ensuring that the potatoes and vegetables are fully submerged. Bring the mixture to a boil.

4. Simmer:

- Reduce the heat to low, cover the pot, and let the soup simmer for about 15-20 minutes or until the potatoes are tender.

5. Sauté Cabbage and Kale:

- In a separate pan, melt the remaining 2 tablespoons of butter. Add the shredded cabbage and chopped kale. Sauté until the cabbage and kale are wilted and slightly caramelized.

6. Blend Soup:

- Use an immersion blender to blend the soup until smooth. If you don't have an immersion blender, transfer the soup in batches to a blender and blend until smooth. Be cautious when blending hot liquids.

7. Combine Cabbage and Kale:

- Stir in the sautéed cabbage and kale into the blended soup.

8. Add Milk or Cream:

- Pour in the milk or cream, stirring to combine. Season the soup with salt and pepper to taste.

9. Garnish and Serve:

- Ladle the Colcannon Soup into bowls. Garnish with chopped fresh chives or green onions.

10. Enjoy:

- Serve the Colcannon Soup hot and savor the comforting flavors of this Irish classic.

Tips:

- You can add crispy bacon bits as a garnish for added flavor and texture.
- Experiment with different types of potatoes for variations in texture and taste.

Colcannon Soup is a wonderful fusion of Irish flavors, combining the essence of colcannon with the warmth of a hearty soup. It's a perfect dish for celebrating Irish cuisine and enjoying a bowl of comfort.

Savory Pies:

Traditional Steak and Guinness Pie:

Ingredients:

For the Filling:

- 2 pounds (about 900g) stewing beef, cubed
- Salt and black pepper to taste
- 3 tablespoons all-purpose flour
- 2 tablespoons vegetable oil
- 1 large onion, finely chopped
- 2 cloves garlic, minced
- 2 carrots, diced
- 2 celery stalks, diced
- 1 can (14.9 oz) Guinness stout
- 2 cups beef broth
- 2 tablespoons tomato paste
- 2 tablespoons Worcestershire sauce
- 2 teaspoons dried thyme
- 2 bay leaves

For the Pastry:

- 2 sheets of store-bought puff pastry (thawed if frozen)
- 1 egg, beaten (for egg wash)

Instructions:

1. Preheat the Oven:

- Preheat your oven to 375°F (190°C).

2. Season and Coat Beef:

   - Season the cubed beef with salt and pepper. Toss the beef in flour until well coated.

3. Brown the Beef:

   - In a large oven-safe pot, heat the vegetable oil over medium-high heat. Brown the beef cubes in batches, ensuring they are well-seared on all sides. Set aside the browned beef.

4. Sauté Vegetables:

   - In the same pot, add chopped onion, minced garlic, diced carrots, and diced celery. Sauté until the vegetables are softened.

5. Deglaze with Guinness:

   - Pour in the Guinness stout to deglaze the pot, scraping up any browned bits from the bottom.

6. Add Remaining Ingredients:

   - Return the browned beef to the pot. Add beef broth, tomato paste, Worcestershire sauce, dried thyme, and bay leaves. Stir to combine.

7. Simmer:

- Bring the mixture to a simmer. Cover the pot and transfer it to the preheated oven. Allow it to cook for about 2 to 2.5 hours or until the beef is tender and the flavors meld.

8. Prepare the Pastry:

- While the filling cooks, roll out the puff pastry sheets on a lightly floured surface. Cut one sheet to fit the base of your pie dish and the other for the top.

9. Assemble the Pie:

- Once the filling is done, remove the bay leaves. Pour the filling into the pie dish. Place the second pastry sheet over the top, sealing the edges. Cut a few slits on the top to allow steam to escape.

10. Egg Wash:

- Brush the top of the pastry with beaten egg to give it a golden finish.

11. Bake:

- Bake the Steak and Guinness Pie in the preheated oven for about 25-30 minutes or until the pastry is puffed and golden brown.

12. Serve:

- Allow the pie to cool slightly before serving. Serve slices of the pie with your favorite sides, such as mashed potatoes and peas.

Enjoy the rich and savory flavors of this classic Steak and Guinness Pie, a hearty and comforting dish perfect for any Irish-inspired meal.

Chicken and Mushroom Pie:

Ingredients:

For the Filling:

- 1.5 pounds (about 680g) boneless, skinless chicken breasts or thighs, cut into bite-sized pieces
- Salt and black pepper to taste
- 2 tablespoons olive oil
- 1 onion, finely chopped
- 2 cloves garlic, minced
- 8 oz (about 225g) mushrooms, sliced
- 1/4 cup all-purpose flour
- 1 cup chicken broth
- 1 cup milk or cream
- 1 teaspoon dried thyme
- 1 teaspoon dried rosemary
- 1 cup frozen peas (optional)
- Fresh parsley, chopped, for garnish

For the Pastry:

- 2 sheets of store-bought puff pastry (thawed if frozen)
- 1 egg, beaten (for egg wash)

Instructions:

1. Preheat the Oven:

- Preheat your oven to 400°F (200°C).

2. Season and Sear Chicken:

- Season the chicken pieces with salt and black pepper. In a large skillet, heat olive oil over medium-high heat. Sear the chicken until browned on all sides. Remove the chicken from the skillet and set aside.

3. Sauté Vegetables:

- In the same skillet, add chopped onion, minced garlic, and sliced mushrooms. Sauté until the mushrooms release their moisture and the onions are softened.

4. Make the Roux:

    - Sprinkle flour over the sautéed vegetables and stir to create a roux. Cook for a couple of minutes to eliminate the raw flour taste.

5. Add Liquid:

    - Gradually pour in the chicken broth and milk or cream, stirring constantly to avoid lumps. Continue stirring until the mixture thickens.

6. Season:

    - Add dried thyme, dried rosemary, and the seared chicken back to the skillet. Stir to combine. If using frozen peas, add them at this stage.

7. Simmer:

    - Allow the mixture to simmer until the chicken is cooked through and the flavors meld. Adjust the seasoning if needed.

8. Prepare the Pastry:

    - While the filling simmers, roll out the puff pastry sheets on a lightly floured surface. Cut one sheet to fit the base of your pie dish and the other for the top.

9. Assemble the Pie:

    - Once the filling is done, pour it into the pie dish. Place the second pastry sheet over the top, sealing the edges. Cut a few slits on the top to allow steam to escape.

10. Egg Wash:

    - Brush the top of the pastry with beaten egg to give it a golden finish.

11. Bake:

- Bake the Chicken and Mushroom Pie in the preheated oven for about 25-30 minutes or until the pastry is puffed and golden brown.

12. Serve:

- Allow the pie to cool slightly before serving. Garnish with chopped fresh parsley and serve slices with your favorite sides.

Enjoy this delicious Chicken and Mushroom Pie, a comforting and hearty dish perfect for a family dinner or special occasions.

Irish Lamb Pie:

Ingredients:

For the Filling:

- 2 pounds (about 900g) lamb shoulder, diced
- Salt and black pepper to taste
- 3 tablespoons olive oil
- 1 onion, finely chopped
- 2 cloves garlic, minced
- 2 carrots, diced
- 2 celery stalks, diced
- 1 cup frozen peas
- 2 tablespoons all-purpose flour
- 2 cups beef or lamb broth
- 1 cup red wine (optional)
- 2 tablespoons tomato paste
- 2 teaspoons dried thyme
- 2 bay leaves

For the Pastry:

- 2 sheets of store-bought puff pastry (thawed if frozen)
- 1 egg, beaten (for egg wash)

Instructions:

1. Preheat the Oven:

- Preheat your oven to 400°F (200°C).

2. Season and Sear Lamb:

- Season the lamb cubes with salt and black pepper. In a large skillet, heat olive oil over medium-high heat. Sear the lamb until browned on all sides. Remove the lamb from the skillet and set aside.

3. Sauté Vegetables:

- In the same skillet, add chopped onion, minced garlic, diced carrots, and diced celery. Sauté until the vegetables are softened.

4. Make the Gravy:

- Sprinkle flour over the sautéed vegetables and stir to create a roux. Cook for a couple of minutes to eliminate the raw flour taste.

5. Add Liquid:

- Gradually pour in the beef or lamb broth and red wine (if using), stirring constantly to avoid lumps. Add tomato paste, dried thyme, and bay leaves. Stir to combine.

6. Add Lamb Back:

- Return the browned lamb to the skillet. Stir to combine. Allow the mixture to simmer until the lamb is tender and the flavors meld.

7. Add Peas:

- In the last few minutes of cooking, add frozen peas to the mixture and stir until they are heated through.

8. Prepare the Pastry:

- While the filling simmers, roll out the puff pastry sheets on a lightly floured surface. Cut one sheet to fit the base of your pie dish and the other for the top.

9. Assemble the Pie:

- Once the filling is done, pour it into the pie dish. Place the second pastry sheet over the top, sealing the edges. Cut a few slits on the top to allow steam to escape.

10. Egg Wash:

- Brush the top of the pastry with beaten egg to give it a golden finish.

11. Bake:

- Bake the Irish Lamb Pie in the preheated oven for about 25-30 minutes or until the pastry is puffed and golden brown.

12. Serve:

- Allow the pie to cool slightly before serving. Serve slices of the pie with your favorite sides.

Enjoy the rich and savory flavors of this Irish Lamb Pie, a hearty and comforting dish perfect for showcasing the flavors of lamb in a delicious pastry crust.

Dublin Lawyer Pie (Lobster and Whiskey):

Ingredients:

For the Filling:

- 2 lobsters, cooked and meat removed from shells (about 1 to 1.5 pounds of lobster meat)
- 1/2 cup unsalted butter
- 1 onion, finely chopped
- 2 cloves garlic, minced
- 1/2 cup Irish whiskey
- 1 cup heavy cream
- Salt and black pepper to taste
- Fresh parsley, chopped, for garnish

For the Pastry:

- 2 sheets of store-bought puff pastry (thawed if frozen)
- 1 egg, beaten (for egg wash)

Instructions:

1. Preheat the Oven:

- Preheat your oven to 400°F (200°C).

2. Prepare the Lobster:

- Cook the lobsters according to your preferred method. Once cooked, remove the meat from the shells and chop it into bite-sized pieces. Set aside.

3. Make the Whiskey Cream Sauce:

- In a large skillet, melt the butter over medium heat. Add the finely chopped onion and minced garlic. Sauté until the onion is translucent.
- Pour in the Irish whiskey, allowing it to reduce slightly.
- Add the heavy cream to the skillet, stirring continuously. Allow the mixture to simmer until it thickens.
- Season the sauce with salt and black pepper to taste.

4. Add Lobster:

   - Fold the lobster meat into the whiskey cream sauce. Stir gently to coat the lobster in the sauce. Remove the skillet from heat.

5. Prepare the Pastry:

   - While the lobster mixture cools slightly, roll out the puff pastry sheets on a lightly floured surface. Cut one sheet to fit the base of your pie dish and the other for the top.

6. Assemble the Pie:

   - Once the lobster mixture has cooled a bit, pour it into the pie dish. Place the second pastry sheet over the top, sealing the edges. Cut a few slits on the top to allow steam to escape.

7. Egg Wash:

   - Brush the top of the pastry with beaten egg to give it a golden finish.

8. Bake:

   - Bake the Dublin Lawyer Pie in the preheated oven for about 25-30 minutes or until the pastry is puffed and golden brown.

9. Garnish and Serve:

   - Allow the pie to cool slightly before serving. Garnish with chopped fresh parsley and serve slices with your favorite sides.

Enjoy the luxurious and indulgent flavors of this Dublin Lawyer Pie, a unique twist on the classic Dublin Lawyer dish, now encased in a delicious pastry crust.

Vegetarian Irish Stout Pie:

Ingredients:

For the Filling:

- 1 cup green or brown lentils, cooked
- 2 tablespoons olive oil
- 1 onion, finely chopped
- 2 cloves garlic, minced
- 2 carrots, diced
- 2 celery stalks, diced
- 1 parsnip, diced
- 8 oz (about 225g) mushrooms, sliced
- 1 cup frozen peas
- 1/4 cup all-purpose flour
- 1 can (14.9 oz) Irish stout (such as Guinness)
- 1 cup vegetable broth
- 2 tablespoons tomato paste
- 1 teaspoon dried thyme
- Salt and black pepper to taste

For the Pastry:

- 2 sheets of store-bought puff pastry (thawed if frozen)
- 1 egg, beaten (for egg wash)

Instructions:

1. Preheat the Oven:

- Preheat your oven to 400°F (200°C).

2. Cook Lentils:

- Cook lentils according to package instructions. Set aside.

3. Sauté Vegetables:

- In a large skillet, heat olive oil over medium heat. Add chopped onion, minced garlic, diced carrots, diced celery, diced parsnip, and sliced mushrooms. Sauté until the vegetables are softened.

4. Make the Gravy:

    - Sprinkle flour over the sautéed vegetables and stir to create a roux. Cook for a couple of minutes to eliminate the raw flour taste.
    - Pour in the Irish stout and vegetable broth, stirring constantly to avoid lumps. Add tomato paste, dried thyme, salt, and black pepper. Stir until the mixture thickens.

5. Add Cooked Lentils and Peas:

    - Add the cooked lentils and frozen peas to the skillet. Stir to combine and let the mixture simmer until it reaches a hearty consistency.

6. Prepare the Pastry:

    - While the filling simmers, roll out the puff pastry sheets on a lightly floured surface. Cut one sheet to fit the base of your pie dish and the other for the top.

7. Assemble the Pie:

    - Once the filling is done, pour it into the pie dish. Place the second pastry sheet over the top, sealing the edges. Cut a few slits on the top to allow steam to escape.

8. Egg Wash:

    - Brush the top of the pastry with beaten egg to give it a golden finish.

9. Bake:

    - Bake the Vegetarian Irish Stout Pie in the preheated oven for about 25-30 minutes or until the pastry is puffed and golden brown.

10. Serve:

- Allow the pie to cool slightly before serving. Serve slices of the pie with your favorite sides.

Enjoy this Vegetarian Irish Stout Pie, a hearty and flavorful dish that brings the essence of Irish cuisine to the table without the need for meat.

Vegetarian:

Vegetarian Shepherd's Pie:

Ingredients:

For the Filling:

- 1 cup green or brown lentils, cooked
- 2 tablespoons olive oil
- 1 onion, finely chopped
- 2 carrots, diced
- 2 celery stalks, diced
- 2 cloves garlic, minced
- 8 oz (about 225g) mushrooms, chopped
- 1 cup frozen peas
- 1 tablespoon tomato paste
- 1 teaspoon dried thyme
- 1 teaspoon dried rosemary
- Salt and black pepper to taste
- 1 cup vegetable broth
- 2 tablespoons all-purpose flour
- 1/2 cup red wine (optional)

For the Mashed Potatoes:

- 4 large potatoes, peeled and diced
- 1/4 cup unsalted butter
- 1/2 cup milk or non-dairy alternative
- Salt and black pepper to taste

Instructions:

1. Preheat the Oven:

   - Preheat your oven to 400°F (200°C).

2. Cook Lentils and Potatoes:

   - Cook lentils according to package instructions. In a separate pot, boil the diced potatoes until tender.

3. Sauté Vegetables:

   - In a large skillet, heat olive oil over medium heat. Add chopped onion, diced carrots, diced celery, and minced garlic. Sauté until the vegetables are softened.

4. Add Mushrooms and Lentils:

   - Add chopped mushrooms to the skillet and cook until they release their moisture. Stir in the cooked lentils and frozen peas.

5. Make the Gravy:

   - Sprinkle flour over the vegetable mixture and stir to coat evenly. Add tomato paste, dried thyme, dried rosemary, salt, and black pepper. Pour in the vegetable broth and red wine (if using). Stir until the mixture thickens.

6. Simmer:

   - Let the filling simmer for about 10 minutes, allowing the flavors to meld. Adjust seasoning if needed.

7. Prepare Mashed Potatoes:

- Mash the boiled potatoes with butter, milk, salt, and black pepper until smooth and creamy.

8. Assemble the Shepherd's Pie:

- Transfer the vegetable and lentil filling to a baking dish. Spread the mashed potatoes evenly over the top.

9. Bake:

- Bake in the preheated oven for 20-25 minutes or until the mashed potatoes develop a golden crust.

10. Serve:

- Allow the Shepherd's Pie to cool for a few minutes before serving. Scoop out servings, ensuring you get a mix of the vegetable filling and creamy mashed potatoes.

Enjoy this delicious Vegetarian Shepherd's Pie as a satisfying and wholesome meal, perfect for any day of the week.

Colcannon Stuffed Bell Peppers:

Ingredients:

For the Colcannon:

- 4 large potatoes, peeled and diced
- 1/2 cup unsalted butter
- 1/2 cup milk or cream
- Salt and black pepper to taste
- 1 bunch of kale, finely chopped
- 4 green onions, chopped

For the Bell Peppers:

- 4 large bell peppers, halved and seeds removed
- Olive oil for drizzling
- Salt and black pepper to taste
- Grated cheddar cheese for topping (optional)
- Chopped fresh parsley for garnish (optional)

Instructions:

1. Preheat the Oven:

- Preheat your oven to 375°F (190°C).

2. Prepare the Potatoes:

- Boil the diced potatoes in a large pot of salted water until tender. Drain the potatoes and return them to the pot.

3. Make the Colcannon:

- Mash the boiled potatoes with butter, milk or cream, salt, and black pepper until smooth and creamy.
- In a separate pan, sauté the chopped kale and green onions in a bit of butter until wilted. Add this mixture to the mashed potatoes and stir to combine.

4. Prepare the Bell Peppers:

- Cut the bell peppers in half lengthwise, removing the seeds and membranes. Drizzle the insides with olive oil and sprinkle with salt and black pepper.

5. Stuff the Bell Peppers:

    - Fill each bell pepper half with the colcannon mixture, pressing it down gently.

6. Bake:

    - Place the stuffed bell peppers in a baking dish. Bake in the preheated oven for about 25-30 minutes or until the peppers are tender.

7. Optional Toppings:

    - If desired, sprinkle grated cheddar cheese over the stuffed peppers during the last 10 minutes of baking.

8. Garnish and Serve:

    - Once the peppers are cooked, remove them from the oven. Garnish with chopped fresh parsley if desired.

9. Serve:

    - Serve the Colcannon Stuffed Bell Peppers hot as a delicious and unique side dish.

Enjoy these Colcannon Stuffed Bell Peppers, a delightful combination of Irish flavors and colorful bell peppers, perfect for a creative and tasty meal.

Boxty with Mushroom and Spinach Filling:

Ingredients:

For the Boxty:

- 2 cups grated raw potatoes (use a variety suitable for mashing)
- 1 cup mashed potatoes
- 1 cup all-purpose flour
- 1 cup milk
- Salt and black pepper to taste
- Butter or oil for cooking

For the Mushroom and Spinach Filling:

- 2 tablespoons olive oil
- 1 onion, finely chopped
- 2 cloves garlic, minced
- 8 oz (about 225g) mushrooms, sliced
- 4 cups fresh spinach, chopped
- Salt and black pepper to taste
- 1/2 teaspoon dried thyme
- 1/2 cup grated Parmesan cheese (optional)

Instructions:

1. Prepare the Boxty Batter:

- In a large bowl, combine the grated raw potatoes, mashed potatoes, flour, and milk. Stir until you have a smooth batter. Season with salt and black pepper to taste.

2. Cook the Boxty:

- Heat a bit of butter or oil in a skillet over medium heat. Pour a ladleful of the boxty batter into the skillet, spreading it out to form a pancake. Cook until golden brown on both sides. Repeat until all the batter is used, keeping the cooked boxty warm.

3. Make the Mushroom and Spinach Filling:

- In a separate pan, heat olive oil over medium heat. Add chopped onion and minced garlic, sautéing until softened.
- Add sliced mushrooms to the pan and cook until they release their moisture and become tender.
- Stir in the chopped spinach, dried thyme, salt, and black pepper. Cook until the spinach wilts.
- If using, sprinkle grated Parmesan cheese over the mixture and stir until melted.

4. Assemble the Boxty with Mushroom and Spinach Filling:

- Spoon a portion of the mushroom and spinach filling onto one half of a boxty pancake. Fold the other half over the filling, creating a half-moon shape.
- Repeat this process for the remaining boxty pancakes and filling.

5. Serve:

- Serve the Boxty with Mushroom and Spinach Filling warm. You can garnish with additional Parmesan cheese or fresh herbs if desired.

Enjoy this flavorful twist on traditional Boxty with the delicious combination of mushrooms and spinach!

Dublin Coddle with Vegetarian Sausages:

Ingredients:

- 8 vegetarian sausages
- 1 tablespoon vegetable oil
- 1 large onion, thinly sliced
- 2 cloves garlic, minced
- 4 large potatoes, peeled and sliced
- 2 carrots, peeled and sliced
- 1 cup vegetable broth
- 1 cup apple cider (or vegetable juice)
- Salt and black pepper to taste
- 2 tablespoons fresh parsley, chopped (for garnish)

Instructions:

1. Preheat the Oven:

- Preheat your oven to 375°F (190°C).

2. Cook Vegetarian Sausages:

- Cook the vegetarian sausages according to the package instructions. Once cooked, set them aside.

3. Sauté Onions and Garlic:

- In a large oven-safe pot or casserole dish, heat vegetable oil over medium heat. Add thinly sliced onions and minced garlic. Sauté until the onions are softened.

4. Layer Potatoes and Carrots:

- Arrange the sliced potatoes and carrots over the sautéed onions and garlic.

5. Add Vegetarian Sausages:

- Place the cooked vegetarian sausages on top of the potatoes and carrots.

6. Pour Broth and Cider:

- In a bowl, mix vegetable broth and apple cider (or vegetable juice). Pour this mixture over the sausages, potatoes, and carrots.

7. Season:

    - Season the coddle with salt and black pepper to taste.

8. Bake:

    - Cover the pot or casserole dish with a lid or foil and transfer it to the preheated oven. Bake for about 40-45 minutes or until the potatoes and carrots are tender.

9. Garnish:

    - Once cooked, garnish the Dublin Coddle with chopped fresh parsley.

10. Serve:

    - Serve the Vegetarian Dublin Coddle hot. It's a hearty and comforting dish that captures the essence of the traditional Dublin Coddle.

This vegetarian version of Dublin Coddle is a flavorful and satisfying dish, perfect for those looking for a meatless twist on the classic Irish comfort food.

Irish Lentil Stew:

Ingredients:

- 1 cup dry green or brown lentils, rinsed and drained
- 2 tablespoons olive oil
- 1 onion, diced
- 2 carrots, peeled and diced
- 2 celery stalks, diced
- 3 cloves garlic, minced
- 1 large potato, peeled and diced
- 1 bay leaf
- 1 teaspoon dried thyme
- 1 teaspoon dried rosemary
- 4 cups vegetable broth
- 1 can (14.5 oz) diced tomatoes, undrained
- Salt and black pepper to taste
- 2 cups chopped kale or spinach
- Fresh parsley, chopped (for garnish)

Instructions:

1. Prepare Lentils:

- Rinse the lentils under cold water and set them aside.

2. Sauté Vegetables:

- In a large pot or Dutch oven, heat olive oil over medium heat. Add diced onion, carrots, celery, and minced garlic. Sauté until the vegetables are softened.

3. Add Lentils and Potatoes:

- Add the rinsed lentils, diced potato, bay leaf, dried thyme, and dried rosemary to the pot. Stir to combine.

4. Pour in Broth:

- Pour in the vegetable broth and add the undrained diced tomatoes to the pot. Season with salt and black pepper to taste.

5. Simmer:

- Bring the stew to a boil and then reduce the heat to low. Cover the pot and let it simmer for about 25-30 minutes or until the lentils and vegetables are tender.

6. Add Greens:

- Stir in the chopped kale or spinach and cook for an additional 5 minutes until the greens are wilted.

7. Adjust Seasoning:

- Taste the stew and adjust the seasoning if needed. Remove the bay leaf.

8. Serve:

- Ladle the Irish Lentil Stew into bowls, garnish with chopped fresh parsley, and serve hot.

This Irish Lentil Stew is not only delicious but also packed with protein and fiber from the lentils and a variety of vitamins and minerals from the vegetables. Enjoy it as a comforting and wholesome meal on a chilly day.

Grilled Delights:

Grilled Irish Sausages with Mustard Sauce:

Ingredients:

For the Grilled Sausages:

- 6-8 Irish sausages (pork or beef)
- Olive oil for brushing

For the Mustard Sauce:

- 1/2 cup Dijon mustard
- 2 tablespoons whole grain mustard
- 2 tablespoons honey
- 1 tablespoon apple cider vinegar
- 2 cloves garlic, minced
- Salt and black pepper to taste
- Fresh parsley, chopped (for garnish)

Instructions:

1. Preheat the Grill:

- Preheat your grill to medium-high heat.

2. Grill the Sausages:

- Brush the Irish sausages with a bit of olive oil to prevent sticking. Place them on the preheated grill and cook, turning occasionally, until they are browned and cooked through. The internal temperature should reach at least 160°F (71°C).

3. Make the Mustard Sauce:

- In a small bowl, whisk together Dijon mustard, whole grain mustard, honey, apple cider vinegar, minced garlic, salt, and black pepper. Adjust the seasoning to taste.

4. Serve:

- Once the sausages are cooked, transfer them to a serving platter. Drizzle the mustard sauce over the grilled sausages or serve it on the side as a dipping sauce.

5. Garnish:

- Garnish the dish with chopped fresh parsley for added flavor and a pop of color.

6. Enjoy:

- Serve the grilled Irish sausages with mustard sauce hot, and enjoy this flavorful and satisfying dish.

This recipe is simple yet packs a punch of flavor, making it a great choice for a casual meal or a barbecue. The combination of the grilled sausages with the tangy and slightly sweet mustard sauce is sure to be a hit.

Grilled Salmon with Irish Whiskey Glaze:

Ingredients:

For the Salmon:

- 4 salmon fillets
- Olive oil for brushing
- Salt and black pepper to taste
- Lemon wedges (for serving)

For the Irish Whiskey Glaze:

- 1/4 cup Irish whiskey
- 1/4 cup brown sugar
- 2 tablespoons Dijon mustard
- 2 tablespoons soy sauce
- 1 tablespoon honey
- 1 teaspoon grated fresh ginger
- 2 cloves garlic, minced
- 1 tablespoon olive oil (for brushing)

Optional Garnish:

- Chopped fresh parsley or green onions

Instructions:

1. Preheat the Grill:

- Preheat your grill to medium-high heat.

2. Prepare the Irish Whiskey Glaze:

- In a small saucepan over medium heat, combine Irish whiskey, brown sugar, Dijon mustard, soy sauce, honey, grated ginger, and minced garlic. Stir until the brown sugar is dissolved and the mixture is well combined.
- Simmer the glaze for about 5-7 minutes, allowing it to thicken slightly. Remove from heat and set aside.

3. Grill the Salmon:

- Brush the salmon fillets with olive oil and season with salt and black pepper.
- Place the salmon fillets on the preheated grill and cook for about 4-5 minutes per side or until the salmon is cooked through and easily flakes with a fork.

4. Apply the Irish Whiskey Glaze:

- Brush the salmon fillets generously with the prepared Irish whiskey glaze during the last few minutes of grilling. Make sure to turn the fillets to coat both sides.

5. Optional Garnish:

- If desired, garnish the grilled salmon with chopped fresh parsley or green onions.

6. Serve:

- Transfer the glazed salmon fillets to a serving platter. Serve hot with lemon wedges on the side.

7. Enjoy:

- Enjoy the Grilled Salmon with Irish Whiskey Glaze as a delicious and flavorful dish.

This recipe offers a perfect balance of sweet, savory, and smoky flavors. The Irish whiskey glaze adds a unique touch to the grilled salmon, making it a delightful choice for a special meal.

Irish Lamb Burgers with Mint Sauce:

Ingredients:

For the Lamb Patties:

- 1 pound ground lamb
- 1/2 onion, finely chopped
- 2 cloves garlic, minced
- 1 teaspoon dried rosemary
- 1 teaspoon dried thyme
- Salt and black pepper to taste
- Olive oil for grilling

For the Mint Sauce:

- 1/2 cup fresh mint leaves, finely chopped
- 1 tablespoon sugar
- 2 tablespoons hot water
- 2 tablespoons white wine vinegar
- Salt and black pepper to taste

For Serving:

- Burger buns
- Lettuce leaves
- Sliced tomatoes
- Red onion rings

Instructions:

1. Preheat the Grill:

- Preheat your grill to medium-high heat.

2. Make the Lamb Patties:

- In a bowl, combine ground lamb, chopped onion, minced garlic, dried rosemary, dried thyme, salt, and black pepper. Mix well until the ingredients are evenly distributed.
- Divide the mixture into 4 equal portions and shape each into a patty.

3. Grill the Lamb Patties:

- Brush the lamb patties with olive oil to prevent sticking. Place them on the preheated grill and cook for about 4-5 minutes per side or until they reach your desired level of doneness.

4. Make the Mint Sauce:

- In a small bowl, dissolve sugar in hot water. Add finely chopped mint leaves and white wine vinegar. Season with salt and black pepper. Stir well to combine.

5. Assemble the Burgers:

- Toast the burger buns on the grill for a minute or two.
- Place a lamb patty on the bottom half of each bun.
- Top with lettuce leaves, sliced tomatoes, and red onion rings.
- Drizzle the mint sauce over the lamb patty.
- Cover with the top half of the burger bun.

6. Serve:

- Serve the Irish Lamb Burgers with Mint Sauce immediately, and enjoy this flavorful and refreshing twist on a classic burger.

These Irish Lamb Burgers are sure to impress with their unique flavor profile, and the mint sauce adds a delightful freshness to each bite. Serve them at your next barbecue or family dinner for a delicious treat!

Boxty Quesadillas with Dubliner Cheese:

Ingredients:

For the Boxty:

- 2 cups raw potatoes, peeled and grated
- 1 cup cooked mashed potatoes
- 1 cup all-purpose flour
- 1 teaspoon baking powder
- 1/2 cup milk
- Salt and black pepper to taste
- Butter or oil for cooking

For the Quesadillas:

- 4 large flour tortillas
- 2 cups shredded Dubliner cheese (or your favorite Irish cheese)
- 1 cup cooked and shredded chicken (optional)
- 1/2 cup diced tomatoes
- 1/4 cup chopped green onions
- Sour cream and salsa for serving

Instructions:

1. Prepare the Boxty:

- In a bowl, combine grated raw potatoes, mashed potatoes, all-purpose flour, baking powder, milk, salt, and black pepper. Mix until you have a smooth batter.
- Heat a skillet or griddle over medium heat and melt a bit of butter or oil.
- Spoon a portion of the boxty batter onto the hot surface, spreading it out to form a pancake. Cook until golden brown on both sides. Repeat until all the boxty is cooked. Set aside.

2. Assemble the Quesadillas:

- Place a flour tortilla on a clean surface.
- Sprinkle a layer of shredded Dubliner cheese on one half of the tortilla.
- Add a portion of the cooked boxty on top of the cheese.

- If using, layer shredded chicken, diced tomatoes, and chopped green onions over the boxty.
- Sprinkle another layer of Dubliner cheese over the toppings.
- Fold the other half of the tortilla over the filling, creating a half-moon shape.

3. Cook the Quesadillas:

- Heat a skillet or griddle over medium heat. Place the assembled quesadilla on the hot surface and cook until the cheese is melted and the tortilla is golden brown on both sides.
- Repeat for the remaining quesadillas.

4. Serve:

- Slice the Boxty Quesadillas into wedges.
- Serve hot with sour cream and salsa on the side.

5. Enjoy:

- Enjoy these delicious Boxty Quesadillas with Dubliner Cheese, combining the best of Irish and Mexican flavors in one tasty dish.

This fusion dish is a fun and flavorful way to enjoy traditional Irish ingredients in a new and exciting way. Perfect for a creative lunch or snack!

Grilled Vegetable Skewers with Irish Herb Marinade:

Ingredients:

For the Vegetable Skewers:

- Cherry tomatoes
- Bell peppers (assorted colors), cut into chunks
- Red onion, cut into chunks
- Zucchini, sliced
- Mushrooms, cleaned and halved
- Olive oil for brushing
- Salt and black pepper to taste

For the Irish Herb Marinade:

- 1/4 cup olive oil
- 2 tablespoons fresh parsley, chopped
- 1 tablespoon fresh thyme leaves
- 1 tablespoon fresh rosemary, chopped
- 2 cloves garlic, minced
- 1 tablespoon Dijon mustard
- Juice of 1 lemon
- Salt and black pepper to taste

Instructions:

1. Preheat the Grill:

- Preheat your grill to medium-high heat.

2. Prepare the Marinade:

- In a bowl, whisk together olive oil, chopped parsley, thyme leaves, chopped rosemary, minced garlic, Dijon mustard, lemon juice, salt, and black pepper. This is your Irish Herb Marinade.

3. Assemble the Vegetable Skewers:

- Thread the cherry tomatoes, bell pepper chunks, red onion chunks, zucchini slices, and mushroom halves onto skewers.

4. Brush with Olive Oil:

- Brush the assembled vegetable skewers with olive oil and season with salt and black pepper.

5. Grill the Vegetable Skewers:

- Place the vegetable skewers on the preheated grill. Cook for about 10-15 minutes, turning occasionally, until the vegetables are tender and have a nice char.

6. Apply the Herb Marinade:

- During the last few minutes of grilling, brush the vegetable skewers with the prepared Irish Herb Marinade. Ensure all sides of the vegetables are coated.

7. Serve:

- Once the vegetable skewers are cooked to your liking and have a delicious herb-infused glaze, remove them from the grill.

8. Enjoy:

- Serve the Grilled Vegetable Skewers with Irish Herb Marinade hot as a side dish or a light and flavorful main course.

These vegetable skewers are not only colorful and vibrant but also infused with the fresh flavors of the Irish herb marinade. They make a fantastic addition to any summer barbecue or as a tasty side for a variety of meals.

Festive Treats:

Christmas Plum Pudding:

Ingredients:

For the Pudding:

- 1 cup suet (beef or vegetarian suet)
- 1 cup brown sugar
- 2 cups mixed dried fruit (raisins, currants, sultanas)
- 1 cup fresh breadcrumbs
- 1 cup all-purpose flour
- 1 teaspoon mixed spice (a blend of cinnamon, nutmeg, and allspice)
- 1/2 teaspoon ground cinnamon
- 1/2 teaspoon ground nutmeg
- 1/2 teaspoon salt
- 1 apple, peeled, cored, and grated
- Zest and juice of 1 lemon
- Zest and juice of 1 orange
- 3 large eggs
- 1/4 cup dark stout or dark beer
- Brandy or rum for flaming (optional)

For Serving:

- Brandy or rum butter
- Custard or whipped cream

Instructions:

1. Prepare the Pudding Basin:

- Grease a 2-pint pudding basin.

2. Mix the Dry Ingredients:

- In a large mixing bowl, combine suet, brown sugar, dried fruit, breadcrumbs, flour, mixed spice, cinnamon, nutmeg, and salt.

3. Add the Wet Ingredients:

   - Stir in the grated apple, lemon zest, orange zest, lemon juice, orange juice, eggs, and stout. Mix until well combined.

4. Fill the Pudding Basin:

   - Spoon the mixture into the prepared pudding basin, pressing it down and smoothing the top.

5. Cover and Steam:

   - Cover the pudding basin with a double layer of parchment paper and a layer of foil, securing them with string. Create a handle by folding a pleat in the center.
   - Place the pudding basin in a large steamer over boiling water. Steam for about 4-6 hours, topping up the water as needed.

6. Cool and Store:

   - Allow the pudding to cool completely before removing the paper and foil. Store in a cool, dark place until Christmas.

7. Reheat on Christmas Day:

   - On Christmas Day, steam the pudding for an additional 2 hours to reheat.

8. Flambe (Optional):

   - Just before serving, warm brandy or rum, pour it over the pudding, and set it alight for a festive presentation.

9. Serve:

   - Serve the Christmas Plum Pudding with brandy or rum butter, custard, or whipped cream.

This Christmas Plum Pudding is rich, moist, and full of festive flavors. It's a wonderful way to conclude a holiday meal with a touch of tradition.

Irish Christmas Cake:

Ingredients:

For the Cake:

- 1 cup (2 sticks) unsalted butter, softened
- 1 cup brown sugar, packed
- 4 large eggs
- 2 cups all-purpose flour
- 1 teaspoon baking powder
- 1 teaspoon mixed spice (a blend of cinnamon, nutmeg, and allspice)
- 1/2 teaspoon ground cinnamon
- 1/2 teaspoon ground nutmeg
- 1/4 teaspoon ground cloves
- 3 tablespoons black treacle or molasses
- 1/4 cup Irish whiskey (plus extra for soaking the fruit)
- 3 cups mixed dried fruit (raisins, currants, sultanas, candied peel)
- 1 cup chopped mixed nuts (walnuts, almonds, or hazelnuts)
- Zest of 1 lemon and 1 orange

For Soaking the Fruit:

- 1/2 cup Irish whiskey

For Decorating (optional):

- Apricot jam for glazing
- Marzipan
- Icing sugar for dusting

Instructions:

1. Soak the Fruit:

- Place the mixed dried fruit in a bowl and pour 1/2 cup of Irish whiskey over it. Allow the fruit to soak overnight or for at least a few hours.

2. Preheat the Oven:

- Preheat your oven to 325°F (160°C). Grease and line a 9-inch (23 cm) round cake tin with parchment paper.

3. Prepare the Cake Batter:

- In a large bowl, cream together the softened butter and brown sugar until light and fluffy.
- Add the eggs one at a time, beating well after each addition.
- In a separate bowl, sift together the flour, baking powder, mixed spice, ground cinnamon, ground nutmeg, and ground cloves.
- Gradually fold the dry ingredients into the butter and sugar mixture.
- Stir in the black treacle or molasses and the 1/4 cup of Irish whiskey.
- Add the soaked dried fruit, chopped nuts, lemon zest, and orange zest. Mix until well combined.

4. Bake the Cake:

- Transfer the batter into the prepared cake tin, smoothing the top with a spatula.
- Bake in the preheated oven for about 2 to 2.5 hours or until a skewer inserted into the center comes out clean.
- Allow the cake to cool in the tin for 15-20 minutes, then transfer it to a wire rack to cool completely.

5. Soak the Baked Cake:

- Once the cake has cooled, use a skewer to poke holes all over the top. Pour an additional 1/4 to 1/2 cup of Irish whiskey over the cake, allowing it to soak in.

6. Optional Decorating:

- If desired, you can glaze the top of the cake with apricot jam and cover it with a layer of marzipan before decorating with icing sugar.

7. Serve:

- Once decorated (if desired), slice and serve the Irish Christmas Cake.

This Irish Christmas Cake is full of rich, fruity flavors and the warmth of Irish whiskey, making it a perfect treat during the holiday season. Enjoy it with a cup of tea or coffee for a festive touch.

Chocolate Boxty Blintzes for Pancake Tuesday:

Ingredients:

For the Chocolate Boxty Pancakes:

- 1 cup raw potatoes, peeled and grated
- 1 cup mashed potatoes (leftover or freshly mashed)
- 1 cup all-purpose flour
- 1 cup milk
- 2 tablespoons cocoa powder
- 2 tablespoons sugar
- 1 teaspoon baking powder
- 1/2 teaspoon salt
- 2 large eggs
- Butter or oil for cooking

For the Chocolate Filling:

- 1 cup chocolate chips (semi-sweet or dark)
- 1/2 cup heavy cream

For Serving:

- Powdered sugar for dusting
- Fresh berries or sliced bananas (optional)
- Whipped cream (optional)

Instructions:

1. Prepare the Chocolate Filling:

- In a small saucepan, heat the heavy cream until it just begins to simmer.
- Place the chocolate chips in a heatproof bowl. Pour the hot cream over the chocolate chips and let it sit for a minute. Stir until the chocolate is completely melted and smooth. Set aside to cool.

2. Make the Chocolate Boxty Pancakes:

- In a large bowl, combine the grated raw potatoes, mashed potatoes, all-purpose flour, milk, cocoa powder, sugar, baking powder, salt, and eggs. Mix until you have a smooth batter.
- Heat a skillet or griddle over medium heat and add a bit of butter or oil.
- Spoon a portion of the chocolate boxty batter onto the hot surface, spreading it out to form a pancake. Cook until bubbles form on the surface, then flip and cook the other side until cooked through. Repeat until all the batter is used.

3. Assemble the Chocolate Boxty Blintzes:

- Take each chocolate boxty pancake and spoon some of the chocolate filling in the center.
- Fold the sides of the pancake over the filling to create a blintz-like shape.

4. Serve:

- Dust the Chocolate Boxty Blintzes with powdered sugar.
- Optionally, serve with fresh berries or sliced bananas and a dollop of whipped cream.

5. Enjoy:

- Serve the Chocolate Boxty Blintzes warm and enjoy this deliciously unique twist on traditional boxty.

These Chocolate Boxty Blintzes are a decadent and delightful way to celebrate Pancake Tuesday or any special occasion. The combination of chocolate-filled boxty pancakes is sure to be a crowd-pleaser!

Boxty Griddle Scones for St. Bridgid's Day:

Ingredients:

- 1 cup raw potatoes, peeled and grated
- 1 cup mashed potatoes (leftover or freshly mashed)
- 2 cups all-purpose flour
- 1 teaspoon baking powder
- 1/2 teaspoon baking soda
- 1/2 teaspoon salt
- 2 tablespoons sugar
- 1/2 cup buttermilk
- Butter for cooking and serving

Instructions:

1. Prepare the Potatoes:

- Peel and grate the raw potatoes. Squeeze out excess moisture using a clean kitchen towel or paper towels.

2. Make the Boxty Mixture:

- In a large bowl, combine the grated raw potatoes, mashed potatoes, all-purpose flour, baking powder, baking soda, salt, and sugar.
- Gradually add the buttermilk and mix until you have a soft, sticky dough. The consistency should be similar to traditional scone dough.

3. Roll and Cut the Scones:

- Turn the dough out onto a floured surface. Gently knead it a few times to bring it together.
- Roll out the dough to about 1/2-inch thickness.
- Using a round cookie cutter or the rim of a glass, cut out scones.

4. Cook on the Griddle:

- Heat a griddle or non-stick skillet over medium heat and add a knob of butter.

- Cook the scones on the griddle for about 3-4 minutes on each side, or until they are golden brown and cooked through.

5. Serve:

- Serve the Boxty Griddle Scones warm with a pat of butter.

6. Enjoy:

- Enjoy these Boxty Griddle Scones as a delicious and traditional treat for St. Brigid's Day or any breakfast or brunch occasion.

These scones have a unique texture and flavor thanks to the combination of raw and mashed potatoes. They are perfect when served warm with a bit of butter.

Irish Halloween Barmbrack:

Ingredients:

- 2 cups mixed dried fruit (raisins, currants, sultanas)
- 1 1/2 cups strong black tea
- 1/4 cup Irish whiskey (optional)
- 3 cups all-purpose flour
- 1 teaspoon baking powder
- 1 teaspoon mixed spice (a blend of cinnamon, nutmeg, and allspice)
- 1/2 teaspoon ground cinnamon
- 1/2 teaspoon ground nutmeg
- 1/4 teaspoon ground cloves
- 1 cup brown sugar
- 1 large egg, beaten
- Ring and/or coin (cleaned and wrapped in parchment paper)
- Butter for greasing
- Honey for glazing

Instructions:

1. Soak the Dried Fruit:

- Place the mixed dried fruit in a bowl. Pour hot black tea and Irish whiskey over the dried fruit. Allow it to soak overnight or for at least a few hours until the fruit is plump.

2. Preheat the Oven:

- Preheat your oven to 350°F (180°C). Grease and line a round cake tin.

3. Make the Barmbrack:

- In a large bowl, sift together the flour, baking powder, mixed spice, ground cinnamon, ground nutmeg, and ground cloves.
- Add the brown sugar and soaked dried fruit (including any remaining liquid) to the dry ingredients. Mix well.
- Stir in the beaten egg until the mixture comes together into a thick batter.

4. Add the Hidden Objects:

   - Carefully fold in the cleaned ring and/or coin into the batter. Make sure they are well distributed.

5. Bake:

   - Transfer the batter to the prepared cake tin, smoothing the top.
   - Bake in the preheated oven for about 1 to 1.5 hours or until a skewer inserted into the center comes out clean.

6. Glaze:

   - While the barmbrack is still warm, brush the top with honey for a glossy finish.

7. Cool:

   - Allow the barmbrack to cool in the tin for 15-20 minutes before transferring it to a wire rack to cool completely.

8. Serve:

   - Once cooled, slice and serve the Irish Halloween Barmbrack. Check carefully for the hidden objects before serving.

9. Enjoy:

   - Enjoy the traditional Irish Halloween Barmbrack with a cup of tea or coffee.

Irish Halloween Barmbrack is not only a delicious fruitcake but also adds a fun and traditional element to Halloween celebrations. Be sure to warn your guests about the hidden objects before they dive in!

www.ingramcontent.com/pod-product-compliance
Lightning Source LLC
LaVergne TN
LVHW072125060526
838201LV00071B/4979